The Island of the Mighty

The Island of the Mighty represents a major new contribution to modern theatrical literature. Described as 'a play on a traditional British theme in three parts', it has not yet been professionally performed in its entirety. The three component plays are the result of some twenty years' intermittent work, first by John Arden and later by both authors. The central figures in the sequence are King Arthur and Merlin the poet and the central theme is the relationship of the poet to society. In its vivid interpretation of historical myth, its wide range of stylised theatre techniques, and its radical presentation of political and social issues *The Island of the Mighty* is an impressive fruit of many years of increasingly close theatrical collaboration between John Arden and Margaretta D'Arcy.

The photographs on the back cover are reproduced by courtesy of Roger Mayne and David Hone.

plays by John Arden and Margaretta D'Arcy

THE BUSINESS OF GOOD GOVERNMENT
THE ROYAL PARDON
THE HERO RISES UP

plays by John Arden

SERJEANT MUSGRAVE'S DANCE
THE WATERS OF BABYLON
LIVE LIKE PIGS
THE HAPPY HAVEN
THE WORKHOUSE DONKEY
IRONHAND (adapted from Goethe's *Goetz von Berlichingen*)
LEFT-HANDED LIBERTY
ARMSTRONG'S LAST GOODNIGHT
SOLDIER, SOLDIER AND OTHER PLAYS

THE ISLAND
OF THE MIGHTY

A Play
on a Traditional British Theme
in Three Parts

BY

JOHN ARDEN

WITH

MARGARETTA D'ARCY

Illustrated with drawings by the authors

EYRE METHUEN
LONDON

First published in Great Britain in 1974 by
Eyre Methuen Ltd
11 New Fetter Lane
London EC4P 4EE

Reprinted 1985

© 1973 and 1974 by John Arden and Margaretta D'Arcy

Printed and bound in Great Britain by
Biddles Ltd, Guildford and King's Lynn

ISBN 0 413 30350 0 (*Hardback*)
ISBN 0 413 30360 8 (*Paperback*)

CAUTION

DEDICATION
TO SOME POLITICIANS OF OUR DAY...

Kicking one another to the floor
(Year of 1974)
Neither Heath nor Wilson dares to understand
Green fields of Britain were always someone else's land.
Eat the flesh of Irishman

And Welsh and Scot (and Englishman):
Remain eternally unsatisfied
Though for each dinner-time of power yet one more living
    creature died.
Hold up your extreme hands in moderation,
Usurpers of the imperium of this nation:
Read us your weekly lecture how the blood you spill

Is running only from the wounds of those who were the first to
    kill.
Soft voices are not heard and never were:

Noise must be drowned down with fire and fear:
Attention, yes, is paid to those who shout aloud –
Tear out their tongues, therefore, lest they attract a crowd.

Drive them out of doors
Ease their feet onto the street
Distort them, if they are women, into hysterical wild whores –
Even your own fury, Generals, Lieutenants, by contrast is
    orderly, reasonable, patrician, sweet. . . . . .

CONTENTS

Author's Preface (1) by John Arden

The Tudor educationalist, Roger Ascham, in a Whitehouse-like eruption, denounced Malory's *Morte d'Arthur* as full of nothing but 'bold bawdry and bloody manslaughter', and bitterly deprecated its popularity among students. I first came across this subversive book in the school library on a wet Sunday afternoon in – I suppose – 1945, when I was fourteen. I had recently been studying Tennyson's poem of a similar name as a set-text for what was then called the School Certificate (nowadays, O-levels) and I had found the Laureate's Gothic-revival intensity rather distasteful – it reminded me of the contemporaneous architecture of the school chapel and the pulpit-rhetoric of the chaplain. This gentleman was notorious for conversing with the boys in a phoney hearty athletic manner while, at the same time, running his cold eyes rapidly up and down as an automatic spot-check for nicotine stains on finger-ends and those dark patches under the eyes which were believed to betray masturbatory habits. He would have got on well enough in Lord Tennyson's Camelot, I thought, and would have had Lancelot and Tristram very smartly removed by their parents as a moral danger to the establishment.

But Malory was quite a different matter. The manslaughter, of course, he had in common with Tennyson: but his battles and tournaments were handled with a kind of butcher-shop technicality (when a knight chopped a portion from his opponent's body, you were told what it was – brain or bowel or 'genitour' or whatever) which seemed only reasonable, considering the type of weapon involved; and the gallantry of the men of the Round Table became particularly genuine when related to the real immediate dangers of hand-to-hand fighting in a society where expert medical attention was but rarely available. The bawdry as well was surprisingly direct. Tennyson's ethereal damosels turned out to have received the attentions of the knights much as the young women of wartime England were said to be responding to the desires of the US Army – in those days present amongst us in large numbers.

But the main impression the book left on me was the landscape within which these savage adventures took place. My school was situated in the extreme north-west corner of Yorkshire, practically in the Lake District. Barren benty heathery hills crowded in over narrow valleys which were filled with tangled woods and noisy with the roar of brown rivers among boulders and fallen tree-trunks. It rained nearly every day. When it did not rain the hills could be seen extending for miles in a precise clear blue air, greeny-brown with black patches, dotted here and there with white sheep. Curlews called continually above the mosses. Huddled in some of the river-valleys were small stone chapels, over-shadowed by thick hawthorn trees and often close to the narrow high-arched bridges that inter-mittently carried the winding valley roads from one bank of the stream to the other. The place-names were in themselves suggestive of the wildness of the locality – Black Force, Cautley Spout, Baugh Fell, Briggflats, Winder Fell . . . etc. Although Malory never in-dulged in detailed description of landscape, being, like all mediaeval writers, primarily interested in the *people* of his tale, he dropped throughout the narrative a whole chain of little allusive hints, plac-ing the action in forests, upon moors, beside fords, between 'two holts hoar', or on the strand of the sea. These hints, as I read, were at once filled out in my imagination by the natural features of the Lune and Rawthey Dales; and the remote castles and hermitages of Malory's Britain became reduced to the scale of the beckside chapels and delapidated disused eighteenth-century textile mills which I walked past every day. The grim abrupt manners of the north Yorkshire dalesmen seemed also in keeping with the mur-derous courtliness of the characters of the romance. I was vaguely aware that the original Arthurian legend was concerned more with the decline of the Roman Empire and the Age of Migrations than with the fifteenth-century Wars of the Roses, so the book's chivalric illustrations (neo-pre-Raphaelite, by the water-colourist Russell Flint) did not much affect my mental vision of the recorded events.

A few years later, when I was at the university, I discovered Robert Graves's intricate, enormous, and (to me at that time) extremely disorientating book, *The White Goddess*. Insofar as I could follow Mr Graves's argument with all its complexities of scholarly reasoning and intuitive poetic 'leaps-forward', I came to understand that the 'Matter of Britain' – as the Arthurian cycle was known in the middle ages – had arisen from roots much deeper and far earlier than the culture of even the fifth century AD. A complete buried pre-Christian, indeed pre-Celtic, world was postulated as

surviving, fragmentarily, in the odd illogical anecdotes of Malory
and, if Graves was to be believed, this survival was due to the
dogged and secret persistence of a school of disreputable Welsh
poets who had handed on from one to another ancient rituals,
traditional tribal identities, and significant festal anniversaries con-
cealed in apparently whimsical fairy-tales and 'surrealist' ballads.
These poets had prepared their work under conditions of actual
physical danger – if their occult purpose had been discovered by
the church authorities or the official Christian bardic establishment,
they could have been held guilty of heresy, if not black witchcraft,
and the consequence of such charges at that time, of course, was
terrifying. Malory, naturally, knew little or nothing of this – at least
at the conscious level of his mind. But I have no doubt that the
overtly 'romantic' adventurous treatment of his material overlaid
an inner awareness of its original forbidden nature. This would in
part account for my adolescent excitement upon reading it for the
first time and for my immediate association of the 'hidden' landscape
of the north Yorkshire dales with the equally 'hidden' substratum of
the narrative. Similarly, I wonder if Ascham's irascible hostility to
the *Morte d'Arthur* was not to some extent motivated by a confused
inkling that all was not quite as orthodox and Christian in the story
as the author would have us believe. After all, manslaughter and
bawdry may be found plentifully enough in the literature of ancient
Rome, and progressive pedagogues did not condemn Ovid or
Virgil or Juvenal or Catullus in such terms. Classical paganism
was obvious enough, well-known by students and teachers to be
'untrue', and yet quite suitable as a vehicle for elegant poetic
imagery and grammatical precision. The Roman writers had not had
the benefit of the Revelation of the Gospels, therefore one could
make allowances. But the same sort of mythological apparatus
applied to our own post-Christian history was something else
altogether: and far better left alone.

At all events, the combination of Malory and Graves prompted
me to write a play about the defeat and death of Arthur. It was by no
means a good play – I found great difficulty in relating the political
plot (of jealousies among British generals leading to the breakdown
of resistance to the Anglo-Saxon invaders) to the Gravesian theme
of the survival of pre-Christian cultural and religious practice and
belief. An attempt to achieve this by inserting into the story a
travelling group of minstrels and irregular actors became a kind of

pastiche of the 'player-scenes' of *Hamlet*, and the whole thing was pretty ponderous and pretentious. This was in 1953, and nobody to whom I sent the script was the least bit interested in it. Two years later I re-wrote the play, keeping the main plot, but replacing the irrelevant barnstormers by a couple of poets – Taliesin, who was presented as Arthur's official bard, and Merddin. The latter character was based upon Graves's hypothesis of the vagrant ballad-singer possessed of a certain secret poetic lore. I also introduced a tribe of Picts, votaries of a Kali-like goddess whose totem was the Wild Cat. Since completing the first version of the story I had seen some of the plays of Brecht, which enlivened my dialogue and stage-craft; and also David Jones's World War I epic *In Parenthesis*, which not only increased my knowledge and understanding of the British mythological background, but greatly assisted me in accommodating this material to the military and political realism of the principal theme. By the beginning of 1956 the corrupt chicanery of the Suez Canal War was about to explode upon us: and I was very conscious as I wrote that British Imperialism in decline had much in common with its Roman precursor. This second play on an Arthurian subject proved more competent than had the other one, and I sent copies around the theatre managements with rather more confidence. The Bristol Old Vic rejected it as being too long and too large for their resources, but implied in their letter that it had at least interested them. The Royal Court also rejected it, without comment. This hurt me, because George Devine's theatre was clearly going to be the place for a young playwright to get himself a start, if he was ever to find one at all: but very soon afterwards they accepted my comedy *The Waters of Babylon*, and my disappointment was forgotten. In 1958, by the way, I was working at the Royal Court as a script-reader, and I chanced to turn up the original reader's report on my Arthurian piece. It said 'boring historical play written in phoney verse'.

For the next few years I allowed myself to forget the 'Matter of Britain' and wrote about other things. But it remained at the back of my mind. In 1966 the BBC offered me a commission to write three television plays, to be performed as a trilogy, in colour, at vast expense, on the new channel No 2. A number of these large-scale productions had been embarked upon and many of them were very successful. There was plenty of money, and, under the beneficent regimen of Sir Hugh Carleton Greene, an apparently unlimited artistic freedom. I found it difficult at first to think of a suitable subject: but Margaretta D'Arcy reminded me of my earlier obsession. On thinking it over, it seemed the ideal framework: three Arthurian stories, with overlapping characters and incidents, linked partly by the 'Round Table' circumstances but more importantly by the personalities of three contrasting poets. Through these individuals and their relationship to the historical events of their era I derived the principle theme of the trilogy. Taliesin, as in my 1955 script, would represent the conservative literary supporter of the official *status quo* – but I would attach him, not to Arthur (who had developed into a disruptive figure, both reactionary and revolutionary at one and the same time, and by no means a representative of any sort of *status quo*) but to one of the short-sighted land-grabbing territorial princes who infested the story, and who regarded themselves as the only possible form of legitimate government for Britain, then and forever. My original Merddin-figure became Aneurin, and was not much altered in his character or ideas. The third poet, who had not played a role in the 1955 script, came into my mind as a result of a number of recent experiences. The Vietnam War had already brought about severe cultural revulsion: writers and artists, who had for some years associated themselves with the protest-movement in Britain against the nuclear policy of NATO, and who had, in many cases, been fined and even imprisoned for 'non-violent civil disobedience', were now beginning to feel that all their idealistic display had been in vain: the Pentagon had triumphed and would continue to triumph against anything they could do. Moreover, the Pentagon (and its subordinate establishments in other western countries), which had earlier been seen by such people as a blundering, but, on the whole, democratically-instituted apparatus, now began to take on the sinister appearance of a totally-malignant monster. The liberal-pacifist paper *Peace News*, for example, about this time, announced in a leading article that its editors had now come to the painful conclusion that the United States of America was the greatest single extant threat to the peaceful future of the world. The social-democratic middle-class-intellectual consensus, in fact, went into a condition of crisis. *Encounter* magazine turned out to have had a tenuous but embarrassing connection with the CIA. Universities were suddenly discovered to have been quietly perverted from the pursuit of true scholarship into the production and commercial development of poison gas, torture-equipment, and thought-crime detection techniques. Dissent became subversion, a broad-based-liberal-outlook became the licking of-the-ass-of-LBJ, experimental art became a method of keeping the students untainted by any sort of precise thought, and sexual liberation became the means whereby the younger generation were distracted from politics. Drug-taking likewise was accorded a similar function. In the early stages of this new and alarming climate I began to think about Merlin. The liberal intellectual who no longer knows what is liberality and what is tyranny, who is unable to draw a distinction between poetic ambiguity and political dishonesty, the religious sceptic who continually uses such adjectives as 'profound' or 'crucial' to describe his pointless agonizing over the existence of God, the sexual failure who masks his fear of women by spiteful little rudenesses and overdone cynicism – these were all types, or portions of a type, that seemed more and more in evidence upon the public literary scene. Now Merlin, in the old Welsh legends, was a poet who went mad and ran wild in the woods as the result of 'a great slaughter'. The story has come down to us in a mutilated form only, but is told in full in another version by the Irish writers of the pre-Norman period. The epic of *Crazy Sweeney* admittedly deals with a king and not a poet, but he does make poems: and Robert Graves, in one of his essays, has given an interpretation of the story which fits in very well with my own concept of Merlin. In fact, a few years earlier, Margaretta D'Arcy and myself had begun to explore the idea of making a film in Ireland based upon the Sweeney legend, and had gone so far as to interest the director George Morrison in the subject. But other projects had intervened and we had had to let the matter drop. Now the cultural confusion prevalent in the late sixties induced to me to revive it, and I decided to incorporate the entire Sweeney story into the trilogy as a kind of coda to the defeat of Arthur and the destruction of his Army. The main sources of the other two plots were Malory for Balin and Balan, and Geoffrey of Monmouth for the defeat of Arthur; both of them considerably modified by material and atmosphere derived from the old Welsh collection of legends called 'The Mabinogion'.

This was all rather complicated and took a long time to get together. I didn't finish the three plays until 1969. The BBC had now fallen upon evil days. Money was short and political pressures were heavy. 'Prestige drama' was very much at a discount. Apprehensive lest my plays should be badly presented on a cut-price budget I tried to obtain guarantees from the BBC that the director appointed to them should be someone I could approve. They cut up nasty at this – writers who attempt to dictate the internal policy of the corporation were no longer to be indulged. And anyway, said Mr Savory, the BBC–2 head of drama, (not the same gentleman who had originally commissioned the plays from me) the trilogy was far too long and the sets I had specified were far too expensive: and did I not realize that the whole thing would have to be done on *film*? Indeed I did realize it – I had actually thought that that was what was wanted: but no, times had changed: the script could not be considered in its present shape – so the question of a director was entirely academic. Goodbye.

The same week as I received this disagreeable news from the BBC, I also got a letter from the Welsh National Theatre, who told me that they wanted a long epic play in some way connected with Welsh history, which they could present in a year or two at the opening of a new theatre. I immediately sent them the TV trilogy, asking them if they thought it would fill the bill were I to convert it for stage performance. They said yes, they did. So I promised to get on with it.

Almost immediately Margaretta D'Arcy and I set out for a tour of India. I took the trilogy with me, intending to re-write it in peace and quiet as soon as we were settled somewhere and had had time to look about us. We stayed for a while in the YMCA Hostel in New Delhi, and every morning before breakfast, at about five o'clock when the weather was still cool, I would sit out on my balcony and type away at the text. For the purposes of the BBC I had written in prose and set all three plays in naturalistic locations, as appropriate to the TV medium. I had hoped that the wild landscape of the north of England (where I had first discovered Malory) would serve to provide my stories with both a background and a prevailing mood. When the poets in the plays recited their works I wrote verses for them, but otherwise the dialogue was as naturalistic as the settings. I intended to have most of the scenes requiring architectural backgrounds shot in farm-buildings and ruined mills and the like, in order to give the feeling of a broken-down imperial civilization. A good deal of the exposition of what had happened in the story before the play actually starts was to be presented visually, in flashbacks and co-ordinated montages of stills. It was very much a TV script, in the style made acceptable by such writers as Troy

Kennedy Martin and in productions like *Culloden*. I ought to have realized that this kind of thing could not and should not be transferred straight on to the stage without radical transformation. But I quite failed to appreciate anything of the sort. Where I had written lengthy camera directions describing landscape, weather, and other visual effects, I made the serious error of attempting to convey the same impressions in grossly over-extended passages of spoken prose. This was, of course, totally against all my theories of play construction, and had the result of making the rather thin naturalistic dialogue appear even triter in comparison. I understand now that my obtuseness was due to the fact that I was rapidly going down with a virulent attack of hepatitis, and my faculties were, without my knowing it, seriously impaired. At any rate, no sooner had I completed the re-writing of the trilogy than I fell hopelessly ill and had to go to hospital. During my illness I asked Ms D'Arcy to get the script sent off to Cardiff. She broke it to me gently that the script was no good – and that any theatre receiving it in its present form would certainly reject it. And even if they accepted it and were mad enough to produce it, it would bore the audience stiff. So why didn't I wait until I was sufficiently recovered and then look at it again? I raged against this verdict – but in the end, upon re-examining the script during convalescence, I was compelled to agree. Unfortunately I was still too poorly to attempt any such radical activity as writing three wholly new stage-plays for a very long time – and time was running out. . . .

JOHN ARDEN

Author's Preface (2) by Margaretta D'Arcy

J.A. showed me his 1955 version of the Arthurian story as soon as he had finished it – this was my first introduction both to him and to his writing. I found I wasn't at all interested in the Arthur bit, but the Picts clicked with me. I had read Tennyson and found him heavy and over-lush: I had read T. H. White and found him whimsical. The combination of these two seemed to me to represent the typical 'British culture' . . . I had spent my formative years until the age of thirteen in an enclosed order of nuns, in Dublin: where the atmosphere was one of extreme nationalism mixed with a keen awareness of money. This was during the boom-years for Irish cattlemen, in and after World War II – most of the nuns came from farming backgrounds and so did the pupils. Their fathers were making black-market prices in the meat trade with Northern Ireland. The nuns *never* came out of the convent once they had gone in, except in a curtained car to transfer now and then to another convent. They entered the order at the age of seventeen, which meant that most of them had been last in the world during the period 1900–1922, the years of intense Gaelic revivalism, bitter anti-British sentiment, and religious sectarianism. We were advised to 'have nothing to do with Protestants and on no account to take a swim with them during the holidays'. However, during the holidays, I did mix with people who represented another facet of the Irish independence struggle – in particular I think of Louie Bennett, suffragette, pacifist, and secretary of the Irish Women Workers' Union. Also Helen Chenevix, another pacifist and militant trade-unionist. Both were Protestants. I met Peadar O'Donnell, socialist-republican writer and activist, who had been involved in the Irish working-class radicalism of the twenties and after. I also read Liam O'Flaherty's novels, many of which were under ban. My father had served in the 'Old IRA' during the War of Independence: while my mother came from a poor Zionist family, some members of which were active in the campaign to set up the State of Israel. As a result, I was, from an early age, heavily saturated with illusory nationalism and realistic anti-imperialism. Hence my distaste for British official culture (I knew nothing of British popular culture).

Because Tennyson was a Victorian imperial poet and because T. H. White went out of his way to sneer at Irish Gaels, I failed to realize that Arthur also stood for exactly the kind of thing that I had always supported – i.e. the struggles of the Welsh against English domination.

So when I suggested to J.A. that he should develop his original Arthurian play for the TV in 1966, I did not feel personally involved in the project. But later on, in America, I met George Steiner, who was lecturing at New York University; and who attacked J.A. for writing these plays on mythological subjects, when, he said, he ought to be spending his 'valuable talent on contemporary themes of the utmost importance'. J.A. was very upset by this criticism, as he had always felt the Arthurian cycle to be of considerable contemporary relevance: though he had not, at this stage, entirely sorted out his own understanding of the stories. The natural result was much discussion between myself and J.A. about the application of the legendary material to the events of the world around us.

The material of J.A.'s third play – *Crazy Sweeney* – had however already interested me – I associated it with the extreme unhappiness of many modern Irish poets who suffer from the schizophrenia of Irish society, where the poet receives fulsome lip-service but no patronage. Energies which could be used to bring together individual writers to form a responsible and (because of their talent) powerful section of the community, are diverted towards self-destructive mutual feuding and an élitist refusal to recognize that the poet is part of society and that the contradictions of society are part of himself. Hence the remarkable ease with which the Irish government is able to muffle both the written and the spoken word. In a country which proclaims its poetic traditions through every university campus of the western world, the Offences-against-the-State Act, the Broadcasting Act, and the official censorship of books all testify to the political weakness of the Irish writers as as a body. The original Sweeney story has also much to say about the roots of hostility between literature and religion. The Irish Catholic Hierarchy has always set its face against popular self-determination, both political and cultural: the United Irishmen of the 1790s, the Fenians of the 1860s, the General Strike of 1913, were all viciously condemned: and even today the Bishops spend more time convolving themselves in-and-out of the technical intricacies and moral scrupulosities of contraception than they have ever devoted to opposing the oppression and injustice meted out by ruling classes north and south. They have also done their best to kill the popular amateur theatre in rural areas – during Lent, the season of penance and mortification of the senses, they forbade dancing but allowed plays: under clerical supervision. The rules against dancing have now been liberalized: but the priest still holds sway over the drama. As he is already possessed of his pulpit, with compulsory audience, the theatre at once becomes subordinate, subservient, and inevitably frivolous.

When J.A. fell ill in India and the deadline for the Welsh National Theatre was rapidly approaching, he asked me to help him completely reconstruct his three TV scripts for the stage. I found that India had made me see both Ireland and Britain in an altogether new perspective. For the first time I thought I understood the Arthurian age. A continuous struggle was taking place within the new post-imperial state: tribal, religious and familial loyalties were in constant conflict with the centralized secular administration at New Delhi. We spent some time in Assam. In this once-prosperous corner of the sub-continent, almost cut off and its economy aborted as a result of the Partition of East Pakistan, there were many groups of people in a condition of permanent hostility, suspicion, and sometimes rebellion. The only thing they seemed to have in common was a resentment of the central government. The matrilineal Christian Kashis hated the Assamese; the Assamese hated the Bengalis; the Bengalis looked down upon the Assamese; the Indian Government was hunting the Nagas and the Manipuris, bombing their villages and throwing them into gaol without trial. Add to this the perpetual evangelic presence of the Chinese People's Republic, just across the mountains – only a few years before, in fact, Mao Tsetung's army had marched irresistibly down into the valley of the Brahmaputra, had impressed itself upon the peasants by its courtesy and willingness to pay for its victuals, and then had marched back again. Shillong, the state capital – in contrast to all this – had been an old British administrative hill-station and was still full of reminiscences of the decayed and vanished Raj . . . This year, 1970, was also the turning-point of the Northern Irish Troubles: the Heath government came to power and overnight the image of the British Army was completely reversed. Where some naive people had believed it to be the 'guardian' of the Catholic minority, it now was revealed as an obvious oppressor: and blood flowed in the Falls Road. The unhealed fratricidal wounds of 1922 broke out anew in the Twenty-six Counties. The imminence of British and Irish entry into the Common Market was a prime factor in this atmosphere of insecurity and violent protest. Irishmen in general felt that affairs were passing out of their control, and that the destiny of their communities was manipulated at a distance by rich and powerful political interests. In such times tribal and sectarian traditions are once more thrust up from the dark corners of the memory.

The combination of these experiences and reflections made it possible for me to map out a strong line for the new version of the three plays, emphasizing the 'concrete phenomena' of eruptive social change, and relating the reactions and emotions of every character to this circumstance. I felt particularly that what was lacking in the TV scripts was a sense of precise sociological realism – there was altogether too much importance given to picturesque historical detail and not enough consideration accorded to the fact that even during the most frenzied periods of economic and political disturbance people still have to go on living. Take, for example, the treatment of the Picts. Certainly this nation believed in correct ritual procedure and in their traditional patterns of marriage and inheritance. But the *essential* element in their life must have been their fishing and farming, to the success of which the ritual customs were held to contribute – a means to an end, in fact: to be dramatized as such, and not for their own sake, however theatrical this may have appeared.

The difficulty of trying to find a theatrical form to express these complex but objective ideas to a British audience without falling into too much ponderous exposition was our principal problem. But having seen several Indian folk-plays, performed and devised by artists of the peasant class, and also having attended the Jatra plays of Bengal (which are the productions of professional poets and acting companies reminiscent of late-mediaeval Europe) we began to discern a way. These plays incorporated material of even greater complexity than our own; they very often dealt with Indian mythology and history: the outline of the stories was regularly traditional, but interpreted by each group according to the variance of local custom and historical influence. Yet the style of the staging was simple and direct, the main emphasis was always towards a strong and vivid story-telling, and where the plot became too diffuse for 'dramatization', the action was hurried forward by means of rapid verse-narrative, songs, and instrumental music. It was

finally upon similar lines that J.A. and I re-worked the entire trilogy –
the TV version was scrapped altogether except for the general plot
and the characters – the structure of the scenes was devised to suit a
kind of staging like that which we had seen in India, and the
naturalist prose of the dialogue was replaced by a combination of
song, prose, various measures of verse, and directions for dancing.

Unfortunately the Welsh National Theatre project fell through:
and subsequently I have had no opportunity to work upon the plays
in production, nor to see them in performance – so it remains a
matter for speculation whether the text in its present form expresses
what I hoped it would.

MARGARETTA D'ARCY

Production Notes

STAGING

Whether the play is done on an open or a proscenium stage, a light platform should be erected in the middle of the acting area, large enough for all the scenes to be acted upon it (with the possible exception of some of the crowd episodes). The platform is to be backed by a frame holding a number of backcloths, which are drawn across to indicate the various sequences of the plays. The drawing of the backcloths can be done either by one of the actors on stage, or by a stagehand, whichever is most convenient on each occasion. The convention to be established is that the 'stage-upon-the-stage' is the precise point at which the significant action takes place; actors seen approaching it, or waiting beside it for their cues, can be in or out of character according to circumstances, thereby breaking down any intense subjective/naturalistic/historical/poetical/classical sentiment which may have been begotten in them by: (a) the fact that some of the dialogue is in verse, and (b) the ancient date of the original stories. The audience will thus be confronted with a group of actors and musicians, moving on and off the 'normal' stage area, who one after another climb on to the 'stage-upon-the-stage' in order to present three narratives in as athletic and rapid and light a style as possible. The backcloths are not to be taken as realistic scenery, indicative of particular places; they are emblems of the kind of environment, emotional and temporal as well as geographic, required for each scene. No other properties (other than the hand props, such as swords etc., the dragon-standard, and maybe the odd stool to sit on) will be needed. The posts at either side of the frame should be constructed so that actors can climb up them.

BACKCLOTHS

(1) 'Camp.' A number of tents with soldiers and their equipment crowded all about.

(2) 'Raid.' Some savage-looking soldiers have just killed a number of defenceless people.

(3) 'Fort.' A rectangular, symmetrical Roman establishment, in somewhat disrepair.

(4) 'Woodland.' Bare trees, clustered darkly and thickly together, with animals among them.

(5) 'Ruins.' The remains of a Roman Imperial building, all broken down by bad weather and neglect. An indication that people live among the ruins.

(6) 'Seascape.' Murky water inhabited by strange and perilous creatures.

(7) 'Mill.' A working water wheel adjacent to a dilapidated wooden house.

(8) 'Snowscape.' A dark sky full of snow flakes, with some indeterminate footprints on the ground beneath it.

These cloths should be painted in bold colours and clear lines; no perspective or naturalistic chiaroscuro.

CHARACTERS AND COSTUMES

We decided not to go into these in detail, as a recent attempt at the plays in a London theatre showed us that however carefully the authors lay out their notions, there is no guarantee that they will be understood. Particular descriptions of characters, involving details of dress and physical appearance, are liable to produce excessive attempts by some actors at 'involvement' with their roles in a way that inhibits a clear rendering of the stories of the plays. Some costume notes are provided in the text. For the rest, it is necessary that the characters should be shown to be alive at a time of considerable material scarcity, when clothes would on the whole be made out of wool and linen. The early British were very fond of jewellery, and of bright colours. They were a vain people, but not necessarily well-washed. The weather in Britain is not very hot, and much of the action of the plays takes place in winter and in the north. The science of tailoring was not common – the normal costume for both sexes was a loose woollen tunic of varying length: men would wear trousers, and women too on some occasions. There would be a very clear and observable difference between the dresses of the rich and poor. As there are a great many characters in the plays, it will probably be desirable to have several actors playing several parts. Let them not be too bothered to change their make-up, etc., unduly, and let the clothes be easily put on and taken off. There are no pictures available of the costume of the period which have any degree of accuracy or authenticity. The military gear of Arthur's

Army would probably be based on what was being worn at the time by the Byzantine cavalry. We do not know what the Byzantine cavalry wore, but they should at all events be shown to be well-equipped. The essential precept to bear in mind in dressing these plays is Lenin's famous question: 'Who? Whom?' Who, for example, derives his income at the expense of whom, and how is this demonstrated in their personal appearance? Bear in mind it was a much more *overt* period than our own. People on the whole looked what they were – and talked like it. The acting must be as direct as the period, and the costumes must reflect the same directness. If characters are dressed too elaborately, and aesthetically, the acting automatically slows down and becomes self-indulgent. It is not quite apparent why this should happen, but it does. Twenty lines (averaged out over prose and verse speeches) per minute is a good acting speed for these plays. The use of percussive music, improvised to follow the actors' speech and movements, will increase the pace and give a brisker definition. There is no reason why this sort of speed should be incompatible with precise diction. The only character in the three plays who really needs pauses in his dialogue is the Miller. And even he, when he starts a section of a speech, must go on till the end, without the usual self-indulgent break for the audience to appreciate how well he is acting. During such breaks, the audience of course is in fact being bored – they wish the acting would *begin*.

The dragon-standard carried by Bedwyr is an important property – a long pole with a three-dimensional model of a long-tailed red dragon on top, and a square banner hung from a cross-bar. The banner bears the symbol of the Chi-Rho. A skull with a gold circlet round its brows is nailed to the cross-bar.

MUSIC

The whole play should be accompanied by music. This is provided by two or three musicians who remain on the forestage throughout the production. They should probably have various percussion instruments, perhaps one woodwind. The music is used: (a) to accompany the songs; (b) to back some of the spoken verse speeches – now and then some of the prose too; and (c) to provide a strong rhythm for important pieces of movement and physical action. Merlin, Aneurin, and the Pictish Poet act as chorus, with songs to relate the narrative and comment upon the action. They each should be equipped with a small instrument – a tambourine or the like – which hangs on their belt and upon which they could accompany their own commentary.

We do not claim to be skilled musicians, and the actual style of the music used is best left for further discussion.

DRAWINGS

Playwrights are not stage designers and it is with reluctance that we found ourselves compelled (by the unsuitability of the décor provided for the London production) to prepare a few small sketches – only in black-and-white – of ideas for the backcloths, if only to supplement our written notes on the subject, which proved so lamentably open to misinterpretation. These drawings appear in the playtext published here.

J.A. and M.D'A.

DRAMATIS PERSONAE:

Approximate Ages :

ARTHUR General of the Army of Britain	70
MEDRAUT Arthur's nephew and lieutenant	25
BEDWYR An officer of the Army	55
CHIEF PORTER of the Army's encampment	50
COMPANIONS officers and troopers of the Army	35–55
DYLAN a commander of light horse	25
The PRINCE of STRATHCLYDE	30
The PRINCE of GODODDIN	35
KING PELLAM	50
MERLIN Arthur's Chief Poet	45
TALIESIN Strathclyde's Chief Poet	65
ANEURIN Gododdin's Poet	25
Other CHIEF POETS	50–70
MORGAN Arthur's half-sister	75
GWENHWYVAR Gododdin's sister	30
GWENDDYD Merlin's estranged wife	28
BONDWOMAN belonging to Taliesin	17
BALIN } twin-brothers, noblemen BALAN }	22
GARLON a bandit	35
Some MONKS	20–30
CARADOC a smallholder	60
A FARMER	30
A MILLER	55
A DOCTOR	40
A BLACKSMITH	40
A COWMAN	60
The COWMAN'S WIFE	30
An ENGLISHMAN	25
QUEEN of the Wild Cat Picts	70

AMBASSADOR   her daughter   35
PRINCESS   daughter of the Ambassador   16
WAR-LEADER   of the Picts   60
POET   of the Picts   40
Pictish FISHERMEN   30–40
FISHERMEN's WIFE   35
MESSENGERS, FIGHTERS, PEASANTS, MADMEN, MADWOMEN,
SOLDIERS' WIVES, etc.

The action of the plays takes place in various parts of Britain, early
in the Sixth Century. Several phrases and sentences in the play are
to be spoken in Latin or Anglo-Saxon and the English translation of
these is given at the back of the text.

THE ISLAND
OF THE MIGHTY

Part One

TWO WILD YOUNG NOBLEMEN

Concerning Balin and Balan
and how ignorant they were

To the Reader: *Indications of place, given at the beginning of each scene—Camp, Raid, Fort, etc.—refer to a repertory of eight simple backdrops used throughout the trilogy. These are described in the production notes at the beginning of the play; the authors' sketches for these backdrops illustrate the text published here.*

SCENE ONE

Camp.
Enter MERLIN *in his official dress (a blue gown, gold chain, and white wand).*
MERLIN (*singing*).

    O Christian men, are you aware
    How once an Emperor controlled
    The going-out and coming-in
    Of every man in all the civil world –
    So hard he toiled?

Camp

Around his boundaries he set
A ditch, a wall, a palisade.
The wild men outside were kept
Outside, until one day he was betrayed,
Or so he said.
The wall fell down, the wild men
Did jump across it and then ran
Down every road that led to Rome –
They broke to bits the Emperor's golden crown
Kicked over his throne.

Enter ARTHUR, *in civilian clothes, all muffled up and walking with the aid of a stick; together with* MEDRAUT, BEDWYR (*holding a dragon-standard*), *and* COMPANIONS, *all in full war-gear.*

ARTHUR (*to* MEDRAUT). And this fisherman, he said –?

MEDRAUT. He is said to have said –

ARTHUR. Indefinite, indefinite, why do we get nothing but rumours – we want facts.

MEDRAUT. He is said to have said that foregathering as was his custom with the skippers of other vessels out at sea on the Dogger Bank – they catch the herring, you know, by means of what is called a drift-net –

ARTHUR. We are aware of the methods employed in the North Sea herring-trade, nephew.

MEDRAUT. Yes, uncle. But you see, they meet other boats, from the Frisian side, and exchange their fish, and so forth. And the Frisian skippers told him that upon their coast there are keels being prepared to bring many crews across to Britain.

ARTHUR. Pirates.

MEDRAUT. More than pirates. He said invaders. He said a whole tribe.

ARTHUR. Saxons . . . Which tribe? I want their name.

MEDRAUT. Not Saxons, uncle. English.

ARTHUR. Makes little difference. The one is as bad as the other.

BEDWYR. If it is an invasion, it is the first one for twenty years.

ARTHUR. And like the last one it will be defeated. If it is true. But where are they coming? The Thames estuary once again? If so we should move the Army out of Caerleon and establish a base towards the south end of Watling Street.

BEDWYR. The region of the Chilterns would perhaps be most suitable.

MEDRAUT. No. The fisherman said that their pilots were asking questions about landing places on the north-east coast, between Tynemouth and Tweed.

ARTHUR. That's a bad coast for landing on.

BEDWYR. They've never landed there before.

MEDRAUT. Perhaps that's why they've chosen it. Anyway the fisherman told all this to an itinerant Gaulish metal-worker who had pitched camp near the mouth of the Humber. This man has now come to Caerleon and I have had him for the last few weeks making a new model of stirrup for some of our big war-horses – you remember you approved the idea?

ARTHUR. Did I? . . . Go on.

MEDRAUT. Well, this morning, quite casually, he told me what he had heard. My opinion is that the information is strong enough to be acted on.

ARTHUR. We will act upon it – with circumspection. Two squadrons of the heavy cavalry. And we won't send them to the coast, we will send them to Carlisle. It's a well-built fort with good roads in all directions – that is, if your brother the Prince of Strathclyde has kept them maintained as he should.

MEDRAUT. I doubt it.

ARTHUR. So do I. We have not visited that territory since the last campaign against the Picts – twelve years ago.

MEDRAUT. Eleven.

ARTHUR. You were only a half-grown boy. You rode your war horse for the first time like a crow on the back of a pig . . . Now you are my Lieutenant.

MEDRAUT. It will be an interesting homecoming. Do you think that my brother will be glad to have the Army in his land once again?

ARTHUR. I doubt it.

MEDRAUT. So do I. Even two squadrons eat a great deal of produce.

ARTHUR. We don't send two, we'll send three . . . I am disturbed by this news. Merlin Chief Poet, you write your customary letter to the Prince of Strathclyde requesting permission for my Army to establish its base at Carlisle for the purpose of defending his realm.

MERLIN. Will I write it in Latin, Chief Dragon?

ARTHUR. Why not? We are a Roman Army.

MEDRAUT. Strathclyde does not read Latin.

MERLIN. His Chief Poet does. He will translate it for the Prince.

ARTHUR. Very well. Lose no time.

MERLIN (*at work upon his tables*). I am writing, Chief Dragon.

ARTHUR. And then you can go the north-east coast, on your own. Discover the courage of the people – or their cowardice – I don't know which. Medraut, you know how I want the march to be organized. Let the Captains and Companions have your orders directly.

MEDRAUT. *Iussa tua comprehendo et perficiam.*

ARTHUR. We set forward our banners tomorrow, one hour before dawn.

Exit ARTHUR.

MEDRAUT. One hour before dawn. Advance party to ride ahead of the column and arrive at Carlisle at least one day earlier. All horsemen to carry as much equipment as they can. Remounts and commissariat men are to travel with the baggage train. See that it is provided with a proper escort.

BEDWYR. Wives . . . children . . . ?

MEDRAUT. With the baggage train . . . oh yes, let the Companions bring their families by all means, we are likely to be in the north till the winter or even longer.

BEDWYR and COMPANIONS. *Iussa tua comprehendimus et perficiemus.*

MEDRAUT. *Uterque ad officia – ite!*

Exeunt all but MERLIN.

MERLIN (*singing*).
The Emperor of the world is gone.
But Arthur son of Uther here
In Britain raised his dragon-flag
And trained and led his men to cruel war –
    Romans once more.
In leather girt and steel complete
They rode their horses tall as towers.
With bodily rage and bloody blade
They drove the screaming heathen from our shore
And broke their power.

He has finished his letter and now claps his hands. A MESSENGER *enters.*

This letter for the Prince of Strathclyde. As quickly as you can, you must get there before the advance guard.

Exit MESSENGER *with the letter.*

As Chief Poet to the General my first responsibility is to praise him by means of verse and music. He has had twelve victories, no less; and I have composed songs of great excellence on the occasion of each of them, with much variety of metaphor and alliterative device. Of equal importance, moreover, is the work that I do in rendering his victories possible. I am now to determine the practicalities of defence for the north-easterly regions. The people there are Christian, but wild and rudimentary. I think they will be more afraid of the General's Army than they are of the English. So a nondescript appearance will be the best way into their confidence. (*He takes off his official robes and insignia. He sings.*)
  I go a smiling travelling man
  To warn them of impeding fate
  And lift their hearts with cheerful word ...

SCENE TWO

Raid.

MERLIN. This is most unexpected ... (*He sings.*)
  I find that I have come one day too late –
    Why did I wait?
I wonder if they are all dead? It appears, however, that this is not the invasion but a preliminary descent upon the settlements for the purpose of plunder, and to spy out the land. Nevertheless it will be dangerous for a stranger to be seen here. I don't look like an Englishman – I hope. But if they don't know who I am they might very well take me for one.

Enter BALIN *and* BALAN *with drawn swords.*

MORS
CRUDELITAS
BARBARITAS
HIC EST

Raid

BALAN. There he is – catch him!

MERLIN (*evading them briskly all around the stage*). I don't even look like a warrior, but they are very hot and furious –

BALIN. I have him – I will kill him –

MERLIN (*trying to wriggle out of* BALIN's *grasp*). Will you listen to me speak –!

BALAN. Indeed I will not!

BALAN: Yes, you will – let him talk to us! (*He pulls* BALIN *off* MERLIN. *A brief scuffle takes place between the brothers –* BALIN's *sword flies up, wounding* BALAN *on the face.*)

BALIN. Brother, you have cut open my face! Not even the English did that.

BALAN. As usual, like an idiot, you cut it yourself. Do not weep.

You are a man; if you were not one yesterday, by God it is time
you became one today.

BALIN. If I could have killed only one of the Englishmen –

BALAN. But you did not and neither did I.

We were hunting rabbits on the hill

When from their ships upon our home they fell.

They burnt our house above our father's head

And dragged our sister from her naked bed.

Not one of all our people is left alive.

And we were hunting rabbits on the green hillside.

BALIN. What a good thing it is there is no poet to record our use-
lessness – we would be made a mock of throughout all Britain.

MERLIN. I am a poet and I will not make a mock of you. I am Chief
Poet to the great General and all this in a way is my fault.

If I had come but one day sooner than I did

Your house would not be burnt and your father would not
be dead.

BALAN. You mean you knew this was going to happen? But how
could you know?

MERLIN.

We had our information.

I made a calculation.

Alas, I was too slow.

Tell me, what will you do –

Tell me, where will you go?

BALAN. Our father was a nobleman – he owned a fishing boat and a
little farm.

BALIN. The timbers of the boat were stove in with an axe where it
lay upon the strand. The bloody butchers even cut the throats of
our draught-oxen.

BALAN. I suppose we ourselves are the owners of it all now, but
there is no one left to do the work – what good is it to us?

BALIN. I can see no future but to become warriors and nothing else
– fight the English wherever we can.

BALAN. But where can we? They've gone back to Germany. There
is nobody here to fight . . . You said, the great General. Who is he,
I've never heard of him? Is he a Prince, or the servant of a
Prince – whose war-band does he command?

MERLIN. You have not heard of him?

BALIN. I have heard of no General in this land since the Romans went away from their Wall – and that was a hundred years ago, I do believe. My father told us stories of it. His ancestors, he said, were made to work as slaves upon that Wall. If your General is a Roman General come back again into Britain, I think I had rather fight the English with my bare hands, all alone.

MERLIN. My General is a Roman as far as his methods of war are concerned. In his lineage and language he is both Roman and Briton. By religion he is Christian, and his work is to defend civility and Christianity from one end of the Island to the other. I am surprised you have not heard of him. I have written many poems about his victories in the south. His greatest one was twenty years ago – the Battle of Badon Hill. Against the Saxons. You must have heard of *that*.

BALIN. Oh yes. I have heard of the Battle of Badon Hill – there were man-eating giants destroyed there by a famous hero called Arthur. He had to help him a red dragon, breathing fire . . . But I did not know he was still alive. I did not know that he had verily existed.

BALAN. I thought he had been an old god of the Island, from before the time of Christ. There were many such, you know – their names come down to us through poetry . . . Only twenty years ago – I can't believe it.

MERLIN. You live in so wild a region, it is perhaps not to be wondered at.

BALIN. I am not wild! My name is Balin! I am the son of a murdered nobleman, and I wish to have revenge for his blood.

MERLIN. Then come with me and meet the General. So your name is Balin. Your brother's name?

BALAN. Balan.

MERLIN. You do wrong to say you are not wild. It is wild young men like you that the General needs for his Army – he will teach you how to ride the great horses and then you will be warriors indeed.

BALIN. Teach us how to ride? We have ridden on four legs before we knew how to walk upon two!

MERLIN. Not these horses. They are great war-horses, he brought the breed of them out of Gaul and upon them his Companions ride to the aid of any Prince or other ruler who calls upon him for his help. He is now in the northern parts because he had heard of the threat of the English. You come with me and I will show you – A matter of a little over one hundred mile.

We cross the moorland and the marshes and we look out upon
  Carlisle.

SCENE THREE

Fort

MERLIN.
  Built by the Roman Caesars four centuries past and gone.
  Precise and rectilinear in well-squared blocks of stone.
More than a little dilapidated by now, I will grant you. But still,
there it is. What do you think of it?

Fort

BALAN. It is a most extensive fort indeed and would contain a large force of men. It does not seem to me to be a very comfortable locality. Much in the nature of a prison, I wouldn't wonder.

MERLIN. As to that, we will discover. It is a long time since I was within those walls myself. Shall we proceed?

BALAN. Just one moment.

Before we go down to the gateway of that place
I have more than one question I will throw against your face.
First, if your General is so well-prepared for war,
Why, when the English came to our home, was he not there?
Second, though he may be a good Christian as you say,
To call himself a Roman is quite another game to play.
We are free men in this Island and are not to be commanded.

MERLIN.

You are happy nevertheless to find yourself defended.

BALAN.

By men of our own nation of nobility and respect
Who treat a warrior as a warrior and not as a subject.
That fort is a cruel gridiron where our liberty must burn to
death.

MERLIN.

Young man, the English will be back before your liberty can
take breath.
There is no one to prevent them except the Army in that fort.
You are no good to the Army . . . unless you join it and consort
With your warrior-companions in fit and regular discipline,
Obey your orders when they're given you and make no
nonsense on your own –
You cannot help the Army and the Army cannot help you.
So turn it over in your thought, boy, and determine what to do.

I will take my ease while you are wrestling with your ridiculous scruples. (*He sits down on one side while the brothers argue.*)

BALAN. I will not be commanded! It is not in accordance with the traditions of our people. Do you not remember we are said to have an ancestor who fell in battle against the Romans at the side of Caradoc! It would be dishonourable for you and me to contradict his example.

BALIN. I am old enough to know, I think, that if I do not fight the English, then I *will* be dishonoured. I can find no way to fight the English unless by means of this General.

BALAN. Then go to him and be his slave. For myself I think it much better to avoid all such persons and the misfortune that they bring.

BALIN. That means you are afraid of him.

BALAN. Yes.

BALIN. You are a coward.

BALAN. No.

BALIN. I am going into the fort. If you do not come with me I shall forget you are my brother!

BALAN. Balin – not!

We came out of one womb
Upon the morning of one day.
All our life until now
We have walked in the same straight way.
One day one single tomb
Shall be carved for us both
If God permit.
How can you say
You will be able to forget!

BALIN. It is not difficult to forget a coward.

BALAN. Then I will turn my back on you and go – no I won't! I will hold your hand – I insist that you hold my hand – (*He puts out his hand but* BALIN *strikes it away.* BALAN *puts his hand to the hilt of his sword.*)

BALIN. Ah-ha-ha, swords! I am quicker than you at that – (*He whips out his own sword.*)

MERLIN (*getting between them in alarm*). Stop this – you can't do this – you are young warriors – you are kinsmen!

BALIN. You get out of my way! (*He pushes* MERLIN *who falls down.*)

MERLIN. Young man, I am Chief Poet – you have hit me in the middle of my ribs!

BALAN. We both had our hands on our swords, but only yours has been drawn. Now I am truly afraid . . . I am going on a long journey to find myself my own life – a coward's life, if you will – without father, without sister, without even my twin brother. Good-bye to you, Chief Poet. Good-bye, Balin, you moonstruck moon-calf – did you never hear it said you should never hit a poet?

Exit BALIN.

MERLIN (*getting up and dusting himself down*). If I had not got in

your way you could be a fratricide at this moment. Are you mad?
I prevent you from one offence and right away you commit
another. The person of a Chief Poet is as sacred as an Ambassador.

> By reason of the working
> Of the words within his brain
> He moves among the minds of men
> Like sunlight or like moonlight
> Like high wind or dark rain –
> Changing the visible face of nature,
> He disturbs the proud heart
> Of each perceptive human creature,
> And therefore by all, save unregulated devils,
> He is preserved from mortal evils.
> And his wisdom and his charity
> Are accorded great authority.

Are you prepared to submit yourself to it?

BALIN. Submit?

MERLIN. You had better. I could turn you into a pillar of salt with
one four-line stanza.

BALIN. I am sorry for my violence.

MERLIN. Very good. Do not repeat it.

> And to prevent its repetition
> I put on you this prohibition –
> You shall not strike the first blow, ever.
> Learn to endure and learn to suffer.
> Before you raise your hand
> Employ your mind.
> And then the General will find
> You are a soldier worthy of his trust.

BALIN.

> If I don't pull out my sword
> The blade will rust.
> I will be disgraced.

MERLIN.

> Better a rusty blade
> Than one defaced
> With blood you did not mean to shed.
> Oh – toss your head
> And storm into the fort
> Upon your own –

Soon you will be shown
The truth of what Merlin has said.

MERLIN *sits down again and watches while* BALIN *walks cockily upstage.*

BALIN. Is there a Porter!

Enter CHIEF PORTER.

CHIEF PORTER. There is. I am Chief Porter of the encampment of Arthur son of Uther. Declare your name and your business.

BALIN. My business is not a porter's business and as my name is a nobleman's I see no reason to give it to you. I will declare myself before your General. So open the gate.

CHIEF PORTER. I will not.

BALIN. And why not?

CHIEF PORTER. Because the knife has gone into the meat and the drink into the horn and there is a congregation of guests in Arthur's hall tonight. No one is permitted to enter until morning. Hot peppered chops and a woman to sleep with you shall have if you stay in the guesthouse outside of the walls. But pass by this gate you shall not.

BALIN. I will have nothing of that.

CHIEF PORTER. Do you offer me violence?

MERLIN (*to the audience*). Violence?

BALIN. No . . . But I will raise three screams at the entrance of this gate so that every woman that is with child within the fort shall miscarry and the General shall hear it and you will be punished – and no one will be able to say that I have not behaved with self-control!

CHIEF PORTER. Scream as much as you like at the regulations of Arthur's camp – they are set down to be obeyed.

The COMPANION *drags him off upstage.* BALIN *gives his first scream. A* COMPANION *enters,* BALIN *gives his second scream. The* CHIEF PORTER *knocks him down.* BALIN *gives his third scream. The* COMPANION *drags him off upstage.*

MERLIN. At all events he got in. (*He gets up, picks up his gown of of office, etc., slings it over his arm, and goes up to the* CHIEF *Porter.*) Chief Porter!

CHIEF PORTER. Chief Poet! You are returned to the General, before we expected you.

MERLIN. Yes. I found out what I had to find quicker than I thought. How long have you all been installed then in Carlisle?

CHIEF PORTER. Two days. It has been raining. And that Prince of Strathclyde has not had a roof repaired for ten years, I don't imagine. I have nothing but a sort of tarpaulin stretched over the turret that has been allotted me for sleeping quarters. You will do no better yourself, I think it likely.

MERLIN. That's not so good. Tell me, do you know who was that young man you just arrested?

CHIEF PORTER. I do not. He was most insolent.

MERLIN. And also to myself. He is best off in the guardhouse trampling cockroaches on his own . . . Any visitors for the General? The Prince of Strathclyde?

CHIEF PORTER. Not he. He is in Dumbarton. He has sent his Chief Poet.

MERLIN. Oh, he has?

CHIEF PORTER. It appears that Strathclyde wants the Army to make war for him upon the heathen Picts of Galloway.

MERLIN. And what does Arthur say to that?

CHIEF PORTER. So far he says nothing. He is waiting to hear what the Ambassador of the Picts has to tell him when he speaks with her tomorrow.

MERLIN. Her? It is a woman?

CHIEF PORTER. A most remarkable woman. Tattooed, she is, from head to foot.

MERLIN. Then she will be an incarnate goddess and a princess of their royal house. The most important person they could possibly have sent. But she need not be afraid. There will be no war against the Picts.

CHIEF PORTER. Why not? Strathclyde will have it.

MERLIN. Strathclyde will have what he is sent. The English have already landed.

CHIEF POET. Ah . . .

MERLIN. They went away but they will come back. Will you permit me to enter?

CHIEF PORTER. With pleasure, Chief Poet. (*He stands aside and then goes out.*)

Enter TALIESIN *in his official dress.*

TALIESIN. Most learned colleague, Chief Poet to the General!

MERLIN. Most learned and senior colleague, Chief Poet to Strath-clyde, revered preceptor of my youth!

TALIESIN. Merlin!

MERLIN. Taliesin!

They embrace, formally.

TALIESIN. You are heartily welcome to Carlisle. On behalf of my master the Prince I have made certain that no possible amenity for the comfort of the Army has been overlooked.

MERLIN. You are most thoughtful, dear colleague.

TALIESIN. Our agriculturalists are in a state of suppressed rebellion over the exactions laid upon them for food for the General's men –

MERLIN. – and fodder for the horses, yes.

TALIESIN. You may smile, but it is serious. You see, the heathen Picts who live in Galloway – the Tribe of the Wild Cat, I believe they are called – are threatening immediate war, and if the rural people of Strathclyde are to be further disturbed by –

MERLIN. No. I am sorry, Taliesin, but until Arthur calls his Council of Companions tomorrow I cannot possibly discuss his intentions with you. He may make war upon the Picts, he may not. He has come here to fight the English.

TALIESIN. I had hoped I might have a private word with you before –

MERLIN. No.

TALIESIN. As one Chief Poet to another, you understand . . . Oh, very well . . . The General will already have gone to bed – I will send a servant to conduct you to his quarters.

MERLIN. No. He will prefer I should wait until the morning. At his age it is best for the hours of sleep to be undisturbed. I think I should like to be conducted to my own quarters.

TALIESIN. Your wife is not with you, I believe?

MERLIN. My wife has not been with me for a matter of fifteen years.

TALIESIN. Ah yes. Then you require a young woman? I have taken pains to provide one.

MERLIN. That is most courteous, Taliesin.

TALIESIN. It is my duty, as Chief Poet. You wait here, she will come. If she is insolent to you, beat her. I do. Good night.

MERLIN. Good night.

Exit TALIESIN.

MERLIN (*singing*).
> A poet meets his colleague and
> No word is spoken of their art.
> To praise the verses of the one
> Is to stick a bradawl in the other's heart –
>   Or a red-hot dart.

> But yet there is one courtesy
> No worthy poet dare omit –
> His colleague needs, as he will need,
> Some half-wit girl to stir him to a fit
> Of carnal wit.

Enter BONDWOMAN, *holding a candle. She offers a curtsey to* MERLIN, *who takes her by the wrist, raises her to her feet and looks her up and down.*

Shows a fit and proper deference – that's good. I'm not going to beat you.
> Our savage man Balin tonight
> Alas he will not have the right
> To be led to his bed
> By so bright a candlelight.

He goes out, with the BONDWOMAN. *After a pause, enter* BEDWYR *with the dragon-standard, which he sets upright at one side of the stage, and* COMPANIONS. *One of them carries a pile of cushions.*

BEDWYR. The General will sit there. Make sure that those cushions are properly fluffed out.

Enter MEDRAUT – *in civilian clothes.*

MEDRAUT. Companions, take your places. The General has finished his breakfast. He will be here upon the instant.
BEDWYR. Here he is.

Enter ARTHUR. *He is wearing the full dress of an Imperial Roman General (over his woollen trews and thick-sleeved tunic)*

– a gold-ornamented breastplate, red boots, purple mantle etc. He carries a gilt helmet under his arm. He has left his walking stick behind, and therefore walks with some difficulty. During the scene he moves as little as possible.

ARTHUR (*sitting down* – MEDRAUT *offers to help him, but is waved away*). Companions, you may be seated. There are at least three matters of business to be discussed. One: Merlin has returned from the north-east with news of a raid there by the English. Where *is* Merlin? Two: from the region of Wirral at the mouth of the River Mersey comes a most curious report. Medraut?

MEDRAUT. A rich man, called Pellam, has declared himself to be a King. King of what, I don't know. But he has written a letter to the General saying that God has told him in a dream that the General is Antichrist, and divine retribution is about to fall on all our heads.

ARTHUR. Antichrist – ha-ha – yes. It has been said before.

MEDRAUT. Not quite so directly.

ARTHUR. And then, three: there is this question of the Wild Cat Picts of Galloway. When I am properly accoutred I will send for their Ambassador. (*He is still adjusting the scarf that holds his sword, and the fastening of his mantle.*) I ask again: where is Merlin? He ought to be here.

> MERLIN *and* TALIESIN *enter hurriedly and take their places.* MERLIN *is putting on his official dress.*

You are not punctual, gentlemen. Taliesin: for what good reason does your master my nephew believe that the Picts are about to attack? I was under the impression that the people of the Wild Cat were an enfeebled and poverty-stricken tribe, and no danger to anybody.

TALIESIN. They are heathen.

ARTHUR. So?

TALIESIN. And therefore by nature malignant.

ARTHUR. True. But their strength?

TALIESIN. Has greatly increased since the Army was last in Strathclyde. Their disgusting sexual customs inevitably bring about the birth of great numbers of children – our own Christian morals of course inhibit such indiscriminate fertility. So therefore –

ARTHUR. Have they attacked my nephew's lands or have they not?

TALIESIN. They have gathered their clans together, Chief Dragon.

ARTHUR. And so, I believe, has Strathclyde.

TALIESIN. Indeed yes. For his own defence.

ARTHUR. I think it is time that we heard the Ambassador.

BEDWYR (*shouting*). Have the Pictish Ambassador brought in to the General!

ARTHUR. We are not here, Taliesin, in order to help your master extend his boundaries by force. The threat posed by the English, on the other hand –

TALIESIN. Is not a direct threat to the territory of Strathclyde. The north-east coast is under the rule of the Prince of Gododdin, and we do not understand why you have not quartered your troops there.

MEDRAUT. Because there is no convenient fort. Carlisle is strategically the most advantageous position from which to –

TALIESIN. But my master must have some immediate recompense for your free use of his resources. If he regards these Picts as a danger to his realm –

ARTHUR. That will do! I will decide what recompense your master needs! Good God, I have known your master since he puked up his pap upon the dugs of his ugly nurse! Just because he is my kinsman, does he seriously believe –

> *Enter* CHIEF PORTER.

CHIEF PORTER. The Ambassador from the Wild Cat Picts, Chief Dragon.

ARTHUR. One moment. (*He puts on his helmet and closes the visor. This, after the style of certain Roman cavalry parade helmets, covers the face entirely and is modelled into the likeness of a classical Apollo.*) Let her enter.

> *The* AMBASSADOR *and the* PICTISH POET *enter. They pass across the front of* ARTHUR, *who is standing to receive them, take no notice of him and sit down in the corner. The* CHIEF PORTER *goes out.*

ARTHUR. Does she understand our language?

CHIEF PORTER. She does, Chief Dragon.

ARTHUR (*sitting down again*). Very good. Lady: it is claimed by the Prince of Strathclyde that your people have –

There is a sudden noisy interruption and BALIN *bursts in, past the* CHIEF PORTER, *who is trying to restrain him.*

CHIEF PORTER. I am sorry, Chief Dragon – but he broke out of the guardroom – my men were unable to hold him –

ARTHUR. Leave him be! I know who he is. Merlin has told me. Stand where you are, young man. I shall have something to say to you in a moment . . . We resume. Lady, it is claimed by Strathclyde that your people are preparing war. Is that the truth?

From the recesses of his plaid the PICTISH POET *produces a sword and a bag of oatmeal. The* AMBASSADOR *unwinds the kerchief from her head, spreads it on the floor, and pours out the oatmeal upon it. Then she puts the sword across the top of the pile. All this in a grave and formal silence.*

MERLIN. She scatters oatmeal on the ground to signify that they desire peace. She lays the sword, scabbarded, on top of the oatmeal to remind us that they are ready for war if we compel them to wage it.

ARTHUR. That is not an illuminating answer to my question. Why can she not reply to me in the ordinary way?

MERLIN. This is her ordinary way. Besides, she is an incarnate goddess, and bound to keep to the proper ritual. The man beside her is her poet. He will be her voice. But she has already spoken through the oatmeal and the sword. It was not a message of threat. She has a grievance against Strathclyde – she will now tell us what it is.

TALIESIN. I will tell the Chief Dragon what is the grievance of these people!

ARTHUR. Thank you, Taliesin.

TALIESIN. They do object that the men of Strathclyde should take up arms to prevent their sheep and their cattle being stolen by the Picts – continual raids and robbery, not a farm upon the border is safe!

ARTHUR. I said thank you! It is the Goddess at this moment whom we are anxious to hear.

The AMBASSADOR *begins to make a strange noise in her throat, beating her hands on the floor in a regular rhythm. Her* POET, *after a short interval, starts chanting to the same rhythm.*

PICTISH POET (*chanting*).
>Five hundred udders full
>Five hundred coats of wool
>Lay them in the right hand scale
>And they shall fail.
>When in the left-hand pan
>A mother-naked man
>Wrapped in a briar-bush foot and hand
>Drops blood at prick of every thorn.
>Scale must fail and rooftree burn.
>Finish.

>*The two* PICTS *withdraw and turn their backs.*

ARTHUR. Indeed finish. So interpret.

MERLIN. Not hard. The theft of sheep and cattle is outweighed, in her opinion, by the slavery to which her people have been subjected by Strathclyde.

TALIESIN. A message of threat. I told you.

MERLIN. It depends how it is looked at . . . I think I had better confer with my colleague. Taliesin – if you please . . . (*He draws* TALIESIN *away to the side of the stage where they talk urgently in whispers.*)

BALIN. Picts! It is nothing but barbarous Picts and their ridiculous grievances! General – if you *are* the General, and if behind that cold golden smile you have really the face of a man – Lord General, there is a grievance!

ARTHUR. Ridiculous . . . ?

BALIN. The English have killed my family!

ARTHUR. Yes, I know that.

BALIN. So why do you not help? I was put in your prison, I was –

ARTHUR. You were instructed in the regulations of the Red Dragon Army of Britain. Merlin tells me you were careful to refrain from striking the Chief Porter even though he struck you. That was, we may say, an improvement. You shall be a Trooper in my cavalry and take part in the defence of your land. You are heartily welcome, sir, into this Christian encampment. (*He strides forward suddenly and grips* BALIN's *hand.*) Chief Porter – you have the sword of this young man. You may return it to him now. He will need it soon, I think.

>*Exit* CHIEF PORTER.

BALIN. To fight the English, not the Picts: – good God the Picts are nothing!

BEDWYR. If we decide to make war on them you will find out what they are.

ARTHUR. In the meantime, learn your discipline, hold your tongue: we are in council.

MEDRAUT. If you can call it that. To my mind the word council denotes a general deliberation.

ARTHUR (*going back to his seat*). Merlin, Taliesin! You are taking far too long.

MERLIN. Alas, we are not in agreement.

ARTHUR. Not?

MERLIN. Taliesin maintains –

TALIESIN. Taliesin maintains that the only Picts we have made slaves of are the ones we have captured in the act of taking booty.

MERLIN. Ah, yes, but from whose land? There are noblemen in Strathclyde who insist on grazing cattle upon the hills which the Wild Cat Picts have immemorially claimed as their own. So they claim the cattle likewise. Let the boundaries be respected and then there need be no war.

TALIESIN. But we cannot ask our Christians to remove themselves from heathen territory! If they graze cattle, they also evangelize. They convert the tribesmen upon their lands!

MERLIN (*aside*). That oatmeal upon the ground represents a whole day's food for one family of the Wild Cat Picts. It is a matter of wonder so few of them become Christian, for thereby they would certainly get more.

TALIESIN. Lord General – you are a Christian – and I challenge you in the name of your Faith! If you will not undertake to help Strathclyde against these savages, then Strathclyde has instructed me to say that he will not permit you to remain longer in Carlisle. I had not wished to put this so bitterly but –

The PICTS *have turned round and are listening to this speech.* ARTHUR *observes them.*

ARTHUR. It would have been better had we not been overheard. Look, she does not believe I can resist your importunity. I do not care to have my powers of resistance cast in doubt before the heathen.

The AMBASSADOR *comes forward again. She takes, from the* POET, *a small bowl with pigment in it, dips her fingers in it and draws streaks of white down her face. Then she takes a second bowl and does it again with red. Then she shakes off her voluminous plaid and – in the same movement – pulls away the ribbon that confines her hair, so that it all falls thick about her shoulders. Underneath the cloak she is seen to be wearing a short skirt of catskin with a long fringe formed by the tails; and little else beside jewellery. Her body is tattooed all over, as the* CHIEF PORTER *has already said.*

MEDRAUT. Merlin, what do you think she is doing?

MERLIN. She is preparing a different and more potent importunity of her own.

ARTHUR. I think we need not hear it. I have made up my mind. The Wild Cat People must refrain from attacking Christians already settled. On the other hand, the Prince of Strathclyde must prevent his subjects from any further encroachment.

TALIESIN. No doubt he might do that . . .

ARTHUR. And then we fight no war except against the English. Settled.

MEDRAUT. To everyone's advantage.

BEDWYR. I think she thinks different.

The AMBASSADOR – *who has been kneeling very still during this exchange – now starts to her feet and starts to dance violently, twisting her body and uttering more noises in her throat, like a medium under possession.*

PICTISH POET (*chanting*).
The cat alone upon her furious hill
Throws out her yellow flame
From claws and teeth and tail
Runs round and round
The circle of her ground
It is her ground upon her hill –

AMBASSADOR (*in a screech*).
It is her ground –

PICTISH POET.
It is her ground –

AMBASSADOR.
Her ground alone –

AMBASSADOR and POET (*together*).
> And she will kill –

PICTISH POET. Whoever steps upon one single stone.

The AMBASSADOR *snatches up her scabbarded sword, draws it, and throws it at* ARTHUR's *feet.*

ARTHUR. She must set forward the terms she will accept.

MEDRAUT. And directly, if you please. We are not here to be entertained by your primeval customs.

BALIN (*aside*).
> God but this is a woman of such danger.
> See how the General is tottering with anger.
> Her obstinate defiance will turn his anger into war.
> He will turn his back upon the English
> And entirely disappear
> Into the hills of the Wild Cat.
> My own land will be eaten flat.

The AMBASSADOR *stops dancing and stands still in the middle.*

AMBASSADOR.
> Terms . . . First let the Dragon tell
> Where he found his father's skull.

She begins to walk round the stage in a triangular figure, pausing at each corner to speak a line of her verse directly at ARTHUR.

> Did he cut it from his neck
> With a sword or with a knife
> Or heave up a great grave
> With his pick-axe and spade?
> Did the Dragon leap and smother
> His mother in her bed
> One night or two nights before his father lay dead?

ARTHUR. Skull. Head. Neck. Dead. This has gone too far.

TALIESIN. There is something in this that is not comprehensible. Does she taunt us with sexual impotence, do you think?

MERLIN. I don't know.

TALIESIN. I think you do.

MERLIN. No. We must remember the marital customs of the Picts are completely the reverse of our own. These heathen women

hold the mastery over their men and thus in their rhetoric there
are many obscure allusions.

TALIESIN. You may not understand it, but the General certainly
does. Look – he has his sword out – my God –!

*ARTHUR has suddenly whipped out his sword and now he is stand-
ing with it poised in his hand as though uncertain whether to strike
or not.*

MERLIN. Lord General – no! She is an Ambassador!

ARTHUR. Ah . . . ! (*He puts his sword abruptly back into the sheath,
but with an awkwardness, so that it goes in at an angle and he cannot
immediately ram it home. He fumbles with it and staggers on his feet.*)

The AMBASSADOR *meanwhile has continued her triangular
progress in silence – except for a constant rhythmic grunting. Now
she stops, stands opposite* ARTHUR *as far away from him as the
size of the stage permits and starts to sing.*

AMBASSADOR (*singing*).
    He has a hand that is no hand
    Until he splices steel to it –
    Oh so most truly he can cut
    Where flesh and bone alone could find
    No entry into heart or womb or mind.

She runs swiftly across to ARTHUR, *stops in front of him, lays her
hands upon his shoulders almost as though she is about to kiss him –
then drops to her knees at his feet. She places her hands on*
ARTHUR's *hips and continues her song – softly – looking up at his
vizored face.*

    Yet arms and painted legs
    Were spread out so generous wide
    Even a little eagle could have fluttered safe inside . . .

*ARTHUR has made no move at all. She drops her hands, places
them on the ground behind her, and leans back upon her arms,
laughing.*

BALIN. General, don't be frightened of her. She is a sorceress, but
that's no proof against the valour of a warrior. Look – (*He picks
up the* AMBASSADOR's *sword and kills her with it.*) – it wasn't
difficult at all.

Immediate consternation all round. In the confusion the PICTISH
POET *makes his escape.* BALIN *is seized by the* COMPANIONS.

MERLIN. O you foolish man, you have murdered an Ambassador.

MEDRAUT. Whatever way we look at it now, there is bound to be
war with the Picts. It is a pity, Taliesin, that you should think it
matter to smile at!

ARTHUR. Turn the stupid savage out. He has dishonoured my
Roman command and the whole reputation of Christ. (*He drags
his helmet off.*)

BALIN. Why – you poor old man – I never guessed you were so
near death. I only did it to help you.

ARTHUR. Death – no – not death – spare his life, but turn him out.
Out of my sight – out of my fort – out of my dominion – out!

BEDWYR. Out!

BALIN. This is her sword. I don't want it.

MERLIN. Keep it. It is accursed. Let it stick to your hands till it
grows into your own heart. You have broken your prohibition. Go!

BALIN. He is no more than an old, old invalid who ought to be
wrapped up in bed.

BEDWYR. Out – you half-cut bullock – or I'll bullock you till you
can't tell a cow from a gap in the hedge –

BALIN (*taking his own sword from the hand of the* CHIEF PORTER,
who has only just now come in with it). There you are – this one's
mine . . . O will you look at me, you civil men of Britain – see, I
have two swords. This morning I had none.

Exit BALIN *holding the two swords proudly in the air.*

ARTHUR. King Pellam called me Antichrist.

MEDRAUT. We do not require to talk about *him*. We have a whole
campaign in Galloway forced on us by this morning's work.

ARTHUR (*suddenly recovering himself*). Adapt yourself, boy, adapt
yourself. Taliesin, come and tell me – at once – what Strathclyde
demands for his war. Merlin, come in one hour – no, half-an-
hour, and be told what you are to do about King Pellam of the
land of Wirral. Companions, the council from this moment
stands adjourned.

ARTHUR *goes out with* TALIESIN *and* MEDRAUT. *The others
exeunt severally, leaving* MERLIN *and* BEDWYR.

BEDWYR.

> Chief Poet, for more than twenty years
> To carry this ancient banner.
> Chief Poet, for more than twenty years
> My hand has held the General's dragon-pole.
> The year I first gripped it was the year of Badon Hill
> And for the first time in that year
> There was nailed to it this skull.
> Nailed for an unknown reason
> And now in its due season
> The seed of that reason has grown thick for the reaping-hook.
> I saw the General how he shook
> And wavered on his bent left foot.
> Chief Poet; why did he ever put
> This globe of bone
> Above the marching helmets of his men?

MERLIN.

> You must have asked him at that time.
> What reason did he give?

BEDWYR.

> He said a soldier could not live
> Unless he knew that he must die.
> This sign of death high in the soldier's eye
> He said would make him twice as brave.
> That was the only reason that he gave.

MERLIN.

> It was a reason that you could believe?

BEDWYR.

> I did not question it.

MERLIN.

> But now you do.

BEDWYR.

> Don't you?
> Ah, the General has grown old –
> So much he must have done
> No poet has ever told.

MERLIN.

> Perhaps will never tell.

BEDWYR.

> Perhaps it's just as well.

I do not think
A sideways man like you
Could ever tell a tale
That was completely true.

Exit BEDWYR *with the dragon-standard.*

MERLIN (*singing*).
A sideways man like me. What else?
How could these horsemen ride direct
Unless their road was found for them
By one like me who skulked and lurked and crept
While they all slept?
This very tale I tell you now
Is all as sideways as the rest.
Balin slips out towards the South.
Balan has gone alone with brooding breast
To the north-west.

To Galloway where the leaves fall down
So far from me and from his brother
He gains a red and lonely glen
Where wilder men than he and wildest weather
All come together.

SCENE FOUR

Woodland

One or two PICTS *enter, dragging* BALAN, *whom they bind and fling to the ground in front of the* PICTISH WAR-LEADER – *who has entered from the opposite side with the* QUEEN *and the* PRINCESS, *who are both wearing cat-masks.*

MERLIN (*singing*).
Without one word they leap on him
And tie him up without one word –
They drag him down and drag him in
So vehemently he cannot use his sword
    Or speak one word.

Had he desired he could have joined
The General's Army in Carlisle.
He chose to go alone. He now
Must suffer blows that make his bloodstream boil.
He would like to smile.

BALAN. I have come here as no enemy. Nor a fugitive from crime.
I am a man of bad luck. Or so it seems. If that makes you want to
kill me there is nothing I can do about it. I would be glad to
know who you are and why you give yourselves the appearance
of wild creatures from the mountain side. You are not Christian?

QUEEN *snarls like a wild cat.*

BALAN. No ...

Enter the PICTISH POET. *He looks carefully at* BALAN.

POET. There is a likeness. I think it is not him.
QUEEN. He has come here from the City of the Wall?

Woodland

POET (*to* BALAN). You have come –?

BALAN. From Carlisle – if that's the place you mean. But I was never within the gates.

POET. It may be true what he says. The small man whom I saw had a new wound on his cheekbone – here – and when they thrust him out from the fort I saw that he carried two swords. One of them was the sword that belongs to the Goddess.

QUEEN. Then this is not the man.

PRINCESS. But he knows who the man was. When the finger touched his cheek he understood what was meant.

QUEEN. It could be that they are brothers.

PRINCESS.

> Broad chest, short body,
> No beard, hair like fire –
> Eyes as pale as the briar-rose flower –

POET.

> Just on his cheek a new wound – here –
> And he would be the red dog with the red-stained teeth
> Who tore your quick dark daughter-cat to death
> And brought upon us all the Roman war –

QUEEN.

> Tore my daughter –

PRINCESS.

> My mother –

POET.

> Killed by his brother.

WAR-LEADER.

> Old lady, shall we kill him?

QUEEN. First let him speak and tell us what he knows.

BALAN. Nothing. If my brother has done a murder in Carlisle I cannot be surprised at it, for that is the sort of man he is. He pulled his sword out upon me, would you credit it? He went and joined the Roman Army. The one thing springs from the other, no doubt. You are at war with the Romans?

POET. And with the Christians of Strathclyde. We think that you are one of them.

BALAN. Strathclyde? No.

> The Prince of Gododdin was the cowardly lord
> Whom my father in his foolishness served.

The Prince of Gododdin was the man who raised no hand
To help his own people when the ruin fell on their land.
I am his man no longer, I am nobody's man.

QUEEN.

Nobody's man and your luck is bad.
Nothing to do but chop off your head.
Kill him.

The WAR-LEADER *already has his knife out.*

PRINCESS.

Not to kill him.
I will claim him.
Let him go and walk
Upon the island in the dark.
Thereby he might prove to us
The badness of his luck.

QUEEN.

Child, he killed your mother.

PRINCESS.

No, he did not:
That was his brother.

QUEEN.

The blood is the same.

PRINCESS.

Nevertheless I make my claim –
Old lady, to me this is no game –
My mother is stark dead
And it falls upon my head
By duty and by right
To choose my man to walk and fight.
So, you see: I choose this one.

QUEEN.

You have claimed him – he is yours.
Let him go to the little island
And walk alone upon the shore.

BALAN.

Take a walk upon an island is easy enough.
Would you tell me what for?

WAR-LEADER. Old lady, I have been war-leader of the soldiers of
the Wild Cat for a matter of forty years. For your pleasure, and

the pleasure of your daughters, and now for your granddaughter, so many good men have been killed –

QUEEN. Not for pleasure, old soldier. For our duty to the Goddess –

WAR-LEADER. You are the Goddess.

QUEEN. Oh yes, you know that.

WAR-LEADER. Then I plead in all fidelity and at a time of so much danger, when we need every man we can get – and every young woman – to carry knife or sling or bow-and-arrow – let this custom be abated.

Enter two MESSENGERS (*girls*).

FIRST MESSENGER. Old lady, the soldiers of Strathclyde have left Dumbarton and are marching south.

SECOND MESSENGER. Old lady, some Romans on their great horses have ridden out of Carlisle and are on their way north. Not many of them, but they are big men, they wear heavy protection of steel.

QUEEN (*to* WAR-LEADER). You have had your doubts beneath your rotten tongue for how long?

WAR-LEADER.
   For a year and a day and a very long while.
   I was afraid.

POET.
   The Goddess knows you were afraid
   And because you were afraid
   Upon the pavement of Carlisle
   Her bold daughter has been laid
   In the smoking pool of her own blood.
   I say that the custom is good –
   And for the very danger of the year
   We must keep it true and with no fear.

FIRST MESSENGER.
   The man who fears the custom
   Is also afraid of the war.

WAR-LEADER. Young soldier, that is a lie. And the Goddess knows it is a lie. Do you not, old lady? Bear witness every wound I have received and every wound I have dealt out.

QUEEN. You are not scorned for your warfare – be assured of it. Continue.

WAR-LEADER. You said to kill this boy – I would have done it. But a certain claim has been made for him. In the nature of a sacred mystery. I don't dispute that claim. But if he is to be let live for the benefit of the Goddess, let him also be let live for the benefit of her people. He is a fighter. Before all else, let him fight. In the place where he is most needed. Without doubt that is the battle against the soldiers of Strathclyde.

QUEEN. Profane, but good sense. Will he do it?

WAR-LEADER. Your life has so far been spared. Out of gratitude, will you fight for us?

BALAN.

> I told a Roman poet that I would not be commanded.
> I would fight for my wild liberty
> Until the run of my blood was ended.
> Liberty from those who attacked me
> And also from those who defended.
> I stood alone when I told him, on a hill outside a stonewall fort.
> It seems to me now that you likewise stand alone
> You look for no strength to help you that is greater than your own
> For fear that it should spring back on you, and then are caged and caught.

QUEEN.

> Good. We are Wild Cats.
> And the cat, like the rat, is aware of the trap.

BALAN. I know nothing of your customs. The priests of Christ have told me that your religion is a creature of hell. I don't think it matters.

> So long as you are free
> There is some hope for me.
> Give me back my bright blade.
> I will fight at your side.

QUEEN.

> Not altogether without prospect of reward.
> You know that already your life has been spared.
> All that you want shall be given into your hand
> And after the battle you shall live with us till you die.

BALAN.

> How do you know what it is that I want?

QUEEN.
> If I show you her face
> Will you spit in her eye?

The QUEEN *lifts off the cat-mask from the* PRINCESS, *who comes smiling up to* BALAN.

MERLIN (*singing*).
> She puts her hands upon his arms
> And her soft little tongue flicks out and in –
> O he will fight with the painted Picts
> Until his amorous blood will cease to run
>> And his eyes grow dim . . .

Exeunt all save QUEEN *and* MERLIN.

> I will tell you how they fight – not like
> The power of Rome or blundering pride
> Of Christian swaggerers from Strathclyde –
> But like the mountain cats themselves who hide
> And glowering glide
> Among the rocks and golden gorse
> They wait to spring and then run back
> Into their holes and none can find
> Upon the stony ground the secret track
> Of their attack.

QUEEN.
> Naked and few, half-starved we are whatever.
> How to turn us into Christians no man can yet discover.
> What need do we have of Christ – for we have the red heather
> Wherefrom we can distil our own strong potent liquor –
> Neither your ale nor beer nor wine
> It makes us drunk enough in our good time.

The QUEEN *stands silently upstage. Enter* STRATHCLYDE *on forestage with an arrow in his upper arm.*

STRATHCLYDE. Merlin Chief Poet, what has happened to my warriors!

MERLIN. Strathclyde, I do not know. I was elsewhere when they were all defeated.

STRATHCLYDE. But I was not elsewhere. I was with my valiant

soldiers. We were fallen upon in the dark places of the forest by
the filthy ragged pagan Picts –

Five hundred men marched out with me
From Dumbarton on the Clyde –
But sixty-eight of those brave men
Got back to their own fireside.

And how many of his rigorous Romans were sent by Arthur to
give us help? One. My brother Medraut . . . He came laughing
and jeering at me, and he came by himself!

MERLIN. Surely not entirely by himself?

STRATHCLYDE. He had a troop with him or a squadron or a half-
squadron – I did not count them. Crucifixion of the Saviour – I
was expecting the whole Army! Taliesin brought me promises –

Enter TALIESIN.

TALIESIN. I also brought you a warning you should not trust to
your uncle's promises. How badly are you wounded, Strathclyde?

STRATHCLYDE. To the death, I wouldn't wonder.

TALIESIN. Not at all – it is but a little arrow in the upper part of
your arm.

STRATHCLYDE. Poisoned . . . !

TALIESIN. Do you think so? Lean upon me, my lord, I will take
care of your safety and bring you home to your own place. By
God we have been most abominably betrayed.

Exeunt STRATHCLYDE *and* TALIESIN.
All the PICTS *re-enter, with* BALAN, *whom they carry on their
shoulders and dump enthusiastically on the ground with a great
shout. Drink is passed.* BALAN *is decorated with garlands and
beads. They put bells on his ankles. He is stained with blood – his
own and other people's.*

MERLIN (*on forestage, singing*).
And so the stronger soldiers go
Betrayed, defeated, all in tears.
The weaker ones who conquered them
Have conquered all their weakness and the fears
Of a hundred years.
Their ancient customs now they know
Still serve them well in dangerous days –

And young Balan who served them best
Must learn to live according to their ways
As best he may.
In ambush he had proved as quick
As any Pict with sword and sling,
And now for drunken gratitude
Their gauds and glories on his wounds they hang –
Does he look like a King?

BALAN. King? Me? Ridiculous. All I want is the girl. She fought
beside me in the ambush more resourcefully than I did – God I'd
be dead, sweetheart, but you had your hand under my elbow with
your knife in it and took the throat out of some bloody champion
who came sideways at me like a mad crab. Shall we go and lie
down somewhere, I have had too much to drink . . . You did
promise . . .

PRINCESS. And for the man who is promised to lie down with the
youngest daughter of the Queen – what else should he be but our
King?

QUEEN.
So great is the people's need –
There are cornfields that must grow
There are deer that must be brought
Within range of the bow
There are fish to be tempted into the net –
There are all our starved daughters
Whose secret furrows cry aloud for seed –
We look for a new King to make fruitful the land.

POET.
All that he wants shall be given into his hand.

He puts a sword into BALAN's *hand.*

BALAN. Oh I don't want to have this – no, I've done with this for
today . . .

PRINCESS.
Not so: you take the sword.
That to begin.
Then when you win
You feel my fingers on your skin.

Two GIRLS, *bearing a large cat-mask with a high crown of beads upon wire-work, have come up behind him. They put the mask over his head. Startled, he feels it clumsily with his hands. When he understands its shape he starts clowning about, making little springs and uttering miaows. The* POET *and the* PRINCESS *take his arms and conduct him tactfully round the stage. A mimed sequence follows, illustrating* MERLIN's *song.*

MERLIN (*singing*).
They lead him out as drunk as a dog
They set his feet into a boat
Across the dark water of their lake
Unto their little island he must float
With his blade so bright –
And there he must begin his walk
All stupid slow with staggering feet.
There is one other man who lives
Alone upon the island – here they meet
And they will fight.

BALAN, *having apparently travelled across to the island, now stands alone in the middle of the stage. The* PICTS *are left behind, grouped in the wings and at the back of the stage. The* SACRED KING *enters and confronts* BALAN. *He is dressed just like* BALAN *wearing only a pair of trews, with garlands and bead jewellery hung about him. He has an identical cat-mask, though his is basically black whereas* BALAN's *is white. He walks with a heavy limp in his left leg. Like* BALAN *he wears little bells round his ankles, so the pair of them jingle at every step. He also carries a sword, but it is a big bronze broadsword with ornamentation, while* BALAN's *is an ordinary functional steel weapon. His torso is tattooed.*

POET (*calling from the distance*). If you don't kill him, he will kill you.

The KING *makes a huge swipe with his sword at* BALAN, *who dodges it and laughs.* BALAN *takes some time to understand that this fight is in earnest.*

MERLIN (*singing*).
For a year and for a day he has
Been God and King of the Wild Cat Tribe –
He sees his bold successor come –

His walking death – in vain the poor man tries
To take great strides–
Look at him – he's cripple – you can deal with him so easily –

The fight lasts some time – up and down the stage like a lethal dance. Then BALAN *kills the* KING.

– it wasn't difficult at all.

The PICTS *now crowd back onto the middle of the stage, surrounding* BALAN, *who stands for a moment triumphant, with his foot on the dead body and his sword held high.*

QUEEN. The King is dead, long live the King!
BALAN.
  I put the sword right into him!

The QUEEN *takes the dead man's bronze sword and gives it to* BALAN, *gently removing his own sword from his grasp and handing it to one of the bystanders to get rid of it. The* GIRLS *lift the big mask from his head.* BALAN *is suddenly a little sobered.*

  I had neither seen his face nor heard his voice.
  Could he have once been a stranger like myself
  Who had to fight for his life here without any choice. . . ?
  It is in my mind these people
  Have some customs that are not good.

The PRINCESS *comes up to him, kisses him – and holds out to him a crown made of twisted gold wire with feathers stuck in it.*

PRINCESS.
  King, come with me.
  We will lie down in the golden wood.

She puts the crown on his head. Then she puts her arm around his body, and leads him affectionately away.

MERLIN.
  He walks so easily towards his bed
  He does not know with what pain
  He will walk away from it again.
BALAN (*stopping short as he goes past the corpse*).
  How did he come to be lame?

Exeunt PRINCESS *and* BALAN.

POET (*indicating corpse*).
> Burn this upon the fire.

FIRST MESSENGER.
> The strength and large desire
> That he brought to us all has gone.

SECOND MESSENGER.
> Poor King, he grew so tired.

Exeunt all PICTS, *the* MESSENGERS *dragging the corpse by the heels.*

MERLIN (*singing*).
> I was elsewhere when all of this
> Went on – I will tell you the place:
> The land of Wirral, to the south,
> Where Pellam King has tried to bring disgrace
> To my General's face.

He exchanges his official dress for a ragged filthy old cloak with a hood and takes up a rough staff in place of his long poet's wand.

> I put on rags. I seemed to be
> A minstrel of the rudest sort.
> Under the moon alone I walked
> When on the road Balin came stepping short
> Savage and curt.

Enter BALIN, *with his two swords.*

BALIN. Hey, beggarman – yes, you – I'm talking to you! I am in search of a man – a rich man – he is reported to live in this region, he calls himself the King of it.

MERLIN. Pellam is his name, I wouldn't wonder.

BALIN. I don't know about that. But they told me on the road that he is recruiting soldiers for his war-band. I have two swords and a courageous heart. I will join him if he will have me. Where does he live?

MERLIN. A strong young man like you should not need to sell yourself to some little obscure King when he does not know for what his two swords will be used. Has anybody said to you, for what purpose this King wants soldiers?

BALIN. You mind your own business what people have said to me. I asked you where he lived and that's all that I asked.

MERLIN. The answer is that I don't know – except it is through at the end of this forest – maybe ten miles away, maybe thirty. I am going that way myself singing songs to earn my bread. Shall we travel together?

BALIN. We shall not. A filthy fellow like yourself would detract from my appearance. I am a nobleman and a warrior, and must be recognized as such when I present myself before this King. You don't need to hang about me – (*He has sat down on the ground and is polishing his swords with a bit of rag taken from his knapsack.*) – all I am doing is attending to my gear – and I may tell you I am completely without money, go away.

MERLIN (*removing himself from* BALIN *and addressing the audience*).
Soldiers? This Pellam recruiting soldiers?
    Divine retribution, I thought his letter said,
    Was shortly to fall upon my General's head,
    What God does he worship then
    Who apparently requires
    Such bloody hands as *these*
    To stoke his punitive fires?

Enter GARLON, *calling to someone behind him.*

GARLON. Goddamn you, will you move –! I will not wait here all night for you! Blood and bowels, this bitch is falling dead on me out of sheer aggravation. Does she want me caught and murdered?

MERLIN.
    Here is a pair of hands
    Even bloodier, it seems to me.
    Wait till the one shall tread on the other
    And we shall see what we shall see . . .

GARLON *has also sat down. The* BONDWOMAN *enters, very weary, carrying a big bundle.*

BONDWOMAN. Ah Garlon – I'm worn out. Christ sake, just half-an-hour – let me sit down and rest.

MERLIN.
    Now here is a strange distraction –
    Sweet candlelight in Carlisle –

What can have possessed the child
To walk barefoot two hundred mile
Humping a heavy load
For a rogue who will rail and goad
And not one word of affection?
Will he hit her? Yes, he will.

GARLON has begun to beat the BONDWOMAN, who sees BALIN and cries to him for protection.

BONDWOMAN.
Oh sir, protect me – I shall be killed!

GARLON has his back to BALIN. Becoming aware of him because of the girl's shout, he does not turn round, but whips a big knife out from under his cloak and stabs backward in a very swift and expert manner. BALIN, however, is just as swift and moves in time to avoid more than a slight stab in the arm.

BALIN.
He takes his knife from out his cloak
And stabs to his back
With never a look –
High time so dirty a cook
Was kicked and ducked
In his fly-blown gravy.

The two men are now confronting one another, tense and dangerous. BALIN has a sword in each hand.

I call to your brute attention
You are not getting struck
Without provocation.

He makes a sudden run at GARLON. There is a short and confused scuffle. GARLON loses his knife. BALIN gets him down – holds him down, with the help of the BONDWOMAN – cuts the waistband of his trews – he tosses GARLON the knife again, contemptuously. GARLON tries to get up, but he is stunned and his trews have fallen round his ankles, tripping him up.

BALIN.
Such is the quality of my new restraint
That even a monkey-faced Chief Poet

Could make no complaint –
If he were here, which thank God he is not.
You may jump or you may crawl
Or you may creep or you may squat.
Myself and your young woman
Will walk away on our four feet.

He and the BONDWOMAN *exeunt, laughing.* BALIN *carries the bundle.* GARLON *rearranges himself.*

MERLIN. Don't go after him just yet. He's a very dangerous young man.

GARLON. So am I, if it comes to that. But more secret with it, as he will find in due course. He talks too much before he gets in his stroke – if it hadn't been for the plaid around his arm, I could have finished him in the one try. I will yet.

MERLIN. He has not always been that way. He is teaching himself something. Very slowly – but he learns.

GARLON. You are a friend of his?

MERLIN. I wouldn't say so.

GARLON. You'd better not. You are in danger from me, you know. I could easily kill you and take everything you have, except I don't think it would be much. I am a bandit.

MERLIN. So I see. That pack of yours he took away with him – it was your loot?

GARLON. It was, and I will get it back. And moreover the girl. I met her on a mountain above the headwaters of the Clyde. She was 'travelling' with an old poet who had a paunch like a haystack. He ran away when I jumped out at them, so I grabbed his concubine and came south. I had been hunted in that region – I thought I'd better move my ground. I am on my way now to the camp of this Pellam. He has offered an amnesty to all fugitive men who are prepared to be his fighters. There might be plunder in it, wouldn't you say? Do you mean to join him yourself?

MERLIN. Not impossible. Against whom will he make war?

GARLON. Ah, that he has not stated. But from the secrecy of his preparations it will be no doubt against some great ruler. I don't give a damn which of them, so long as I get in my stroke. Afterwards against Pellam himself, if the chance is offered me – who knows? I have suffered far too much from these Kings and these Princes. Every one of them is my enemy. Though they don't know it till they feel my weapon. *He* would have felt it, but he had his damned plaid wrapped round his arm. A nobleman of sorts, I wouldn't wonder . . . I had a cornfield and an orchard, five pigs, and a black-and-white cow. But the Prince of Gwynedd took them off me, grabbed my wife to be his mistress, turned me out of my cottage. For what reason? I was in debt to him, rent and so forth. Interest upon money lent me. Said I was to be bound to him as a serf for evermore if I could not pay it. My grandfather had been a serf – but there was a Roman Emperor in those days. Not one of our own hereditary Princes. For a Roman it was natural he should enslave the men of Britain. My grandfather bought his freedom with hard work. Died of it moreover. Spitting blood all down the blanket. Not for me. Here's my liberty – (*He flourishes his knife.*) Secret, from behind a cloak. Gwynedd's bailiff had this in his kidneys – ah!

MERLIN. What's your name?

GARLON. Garlon. I don't like you. You let me talk too much because I am angry, and say never a word yourself. I think that in reality you are not as ragged as your cloak. What is your business?

MERLIN. I sing songs.

GARLON. So sing one and prove it.

MERLIN. I will see what I can do . . . (*Aside.*)

> Let me think what stupid vulgar ditty
> Would entertain a lustful man
> Who knows neither truth nor pity . . . ?

Sings bawdily.

> Oh did you ever hear
> And did you hear again
> Of the game that we played
> With the virgin in the lane?
>
> She walked oh so careful
> And she walked oh so neat
> And her little arse went up and down
> Above her little feet . . .

GARLON. Not a good song nor a new one. It was made by a man who never laid hand on a true woman in all his days. I heard it sung by the bailiff of the Prince of Gwynedd the very evening that I killed him. And he intended it to allude to my wife. God help her where

she is. Now here is a song; let me see if you have heard of it. A
song of religion – you could put it that way. (*He sings.*)

    John Baptist out of the desert walked
    And all he wore was a cloth of hair
    And all he could cry was 'Beware beware –
    The naked man has come to steal your coat!'

    He met with Jesus by the river
    And Jesus was dressed in cloth-of-gold
    John Baptist tore it off and left him shivering cold –
    John Baptist's head was served on a dish for the King's dinner.

    Who fetched the King's soldiers to run him in?
    Lord Jesus who was both Priest and King,
    Who forgave the rich men all their sins
    So long as they said that they loved him
    And would whip their people till they loved him too –
    Lord Jesus, a great revenge is coming upon you!

Blasphemy, isn't it? I can read it in your eyes. You hate me and
you hate the song. If you weren't all in rags you would be meat
for my sharp knife. Earn a little more money by singing filthiness
about poor men's wives and I'll stab you in the kidneys and make
away with the lot of it.

    Exit GARLON.

MERLIN. Now that is a man who would be better off dead. Oh, he
will be if he joins with Pellam.

SCENE FIVE

Ruins.

Enter BALIN *and* BONDWOMAN.

BONDWOMAN.
    Oh you are scornful and brave
    But yet you are not wise.
    You would have done much better
    To put Garlon in his grave.

Ruins

He will follow us invisible
And strike from the shadow of a tree
You will be laid dead. He will take back me.

BALIN.

Is that what you want him to do?

BONDWOMAN.

If he does it then he does it.
He will be a better man than you.

BALIN.

How can you say you ever felt love
For a man who treats you like a slave?

BONDWOMAN.

Because until he met with you

I believed that he was brave.
Moreover, I was a slave.
Chief Poet Taliesin did with me what he wanted.
I might well have been contented
Had he now and then made use
Of my beauty for his verse.
But he did not. I was for him
His recreation and that was the end.
Sometimes he would serve me up
Like bread-and-cheese to a learned friend.
With Garlon it was different.
When he was not frightened he would talk.
He would tell me about his wife,
He would instruct me in the rage and craftiness
That a bandit needs to live his life.
But then you met him and you beat him –
And I suppose I belong to you.
So tell me, love, where will we go –
Tell me, what shall we do?

BALIN. Fight the English. Kill all the murderers. Chop their bones and throw them broadcast among the broken seashells of the strand. If Pellam has an army that will be what it is for.

BONDWOMAN. Will it? Garlon told me otherwise –

BALIN. Your Garlon was base and ignorant. This Pellam is a King. He will therefore understand the rights and duties of a man of noble blood.

BONDWOMAN. With two swords . . . ?

BALIN. Correct. And no damn nonsense about the honour of a great Empire that has been three generations dead.

BONDWOMAN. But where we are here it is the coast turned towards Ireland. There are no English here.

BALIN. That has yet to be discovered.

BONDWOMAN.
Look you, we have a great big sack
Full of gold to put on your neck
And embroidered cloth for your strong back.
We have a whole great Island full of trees and mountain water.
And no one to control us wherever we shall wander.
Neither poet nor king knows who or where we are.
In the summer we can lie down bare

Upon the mosses and beneath the briar,
In the winter we can huddle close and kiss each other warm –
A little hut you can make for us out of branches of black-
     thorn . . .
The wind comes cold already –
Why don't we build a fire –
I don't think we can cook any food
But I have some nuts and apples
I found growing wild in the wood . . .
Don't go and be a soldier –
I will love you forever.

BALIN.
No, girl, it's no good.
My father has a ghost, don't you see, he sits inside my head crack-
ing his fingers just here at the back of my eyes. I *must* talk with
King Pellam. If he offers me nothing I swear I'll forget it all and
I'll look for nothing more. Except you, and that's all. Let's have an
apple. What kind of a house do you imagine this was once before
the bushes grew all over it?

BONDWOMAN. House of a great man – some Roman very probably.
Birds live in it, and badgers. End of all great men, so . . .

> PELLAM *enters, accompanied by a* MONK. *He comes in behind the*
> BONDWOMAN, *and as he speaks he softly runs his hand around*
> *her breast.*

PELLAM. My house, girl. Not ended yet. The plaster is cracked from
the bricks, but the symbol of Christ is new painted.

> *He takes a small, brightly coloured, Chi-Rho medallion out of a*
> *fold of his toga.* BALIN *has risen menacingly.* PELLAM *fends him*
> *off with the raised medallion.* BALIN *is nonplussed.*

God bless you, sir. Put down your sword. You are heartily welcome into this Christian land. Of which, through the voices of my
dutiful people, I have assumed the heavy burden of Kingship.
Alas, it is too great for me. I had rather live a quiet life. My name
is Pellam.

BALIN. You? But I thought you would be a war-leader?

PELLAM. Most unwillingly, I am. Compelled by the urging of God,
I must lend my strength against the hypocrites. You are a soldier –
I see you have two swords.

BALIN. I am a soldier and a nobleman and I –

PELLAM. And you will fight like a lion for the integrity of Our Blessed Saviour. You have heard no doubt of Arthur, son of Uther.

BALIN. Heard of him and met him.

PELLAM. He makes war in the name of Christ. But it is nothing; it is hypocrisy. I was told so in a dream. A sweet angel communicated. This holy man interpreted.

MONK. The King's dream was of a red dragon who was struck to the heart by a long black spear. The angel was white and gold and sang to the King in his dream –

PELLAM (*singing*).

Upon the Tree of Cavalry
They hung up God for all to see.
He did not die until He felt
This Roman spear-point in his bleeding pelt.

MONK. And three days after the dream the King received that very Spear.

PELLAM. The most holy relic of all Christendom, brought to me from Syria by a flea-bitten old Jew who did not know its value. Why, he was of no more account than that dirty bunch of lewdness over there. (*He points to* MERLIN *who is huddled in a corner and seems to be asleep.*) I paid him thirty pieces of silver – which I thought a singular irony – do you not agree?

BALIN. I don't understand. If the Spear is as old as that it will most likely break in two as soon as it is used. Worm-eaten, I wouldn't wonder.

MONK. Oh yes, and rusted with the Blood of God.

PELLAM.

Yet it is mine
And it is a certain sign.
The Dragon of Arthur
Is the sign of his own disaster
And that skull with its grinning teeth
Is the mark of his own death.

MONK.

He who bears the Holy Spear in hand
Is God's commander in this Christian land.
Arthur is the Devil's man
And Arthur's regiment is soon to end.

PELLAM. I have already had private assurances of support from so many of the Princes, who are sick and tired of Arthur's pride. He does nothing to protect them and he eats up all their fortune. If I can make war on him and defeat him while he is altogether taken away into Strathclyde's quarrel against the Picts, I do believe these foolish Princes will elect me their High King.

Now there is a future for you. Prove yourself in battle, you could be a Captain of my warband. You could be a greater man than Medraut and he is no older than you. What do you think of it?

BALIN (*to Bondwoman*). What do you think of it?

BONDWOMAN. I think nothing at all of it.

BALIN (*in a furious whisper*). Christ, but you're no help to me – (*He turns back to* PELLAM.) King Pellam, look you here – do you not mean to fight the English? It is only against the English that I have come here to fight. Because the English have killed –

PELLAM. Most certainly we shall fight the English. For what other reason have I been vouchsafed the custody of the Holy Spear of Mount Golgotha? But first things first, young man. Arthur the vile heretic is very near at hand. The English are yet far.

BALIN. Oh no they are not.

MONK. Be silent when the King speaks! Oh, decorum, these wild young warriors have very little of it, I fear.

PELLAM. It is not important. What is important is that he should be convinced of the High Divinity that guides our cause. We must show to him the Holy Spear.

MONK. King Pellam, the Spear is a Sacred Mystery. In God's Name do not be too free in revealing it to the unregenerate. You have already said too much.

PELLAM. I think I can be the judge of that. I like the look of this young man. He is most ardent against the heathen. You come with me. You shall be convinced.

> PELLAM *goes out.* BALIN *is about to take the* BONDWOMAN *by the hand and follow him out, when the* MONK *prevents him. The* BONDWOMAN *is eating an apple.*

MONK. She must not come. She is the greed of deceitful Eve. She will profane the Mystery. Let her wait for you here. She will not be disturbed.

> BALIN *pauses, irresolute for an instant. The* BONDWOMAN *pulls him away to one side and speaks urgently in a low voice.*

BONDWOMAN. For you to help a little King to grow into a bigger one – what good is that to me? Did you not observe where he puts his clammy hand – as though by accident, wasn't it? He will make me the slave of his bed, and you too will be his slave. Look, forget you are a nobleman. If you must live a life of fighting, why not fight in defence of me? There are so many like myself – everything that is ever done in the name of God or good order becomes done against us. The best thing of all would be if you could make friends with Garlon. He is not always clever but he has had dealings in his time with every outlaw gang through the breadth of the forests of Britain. What – yourself and himself – good friends and good fighters – you could soon have a thousand men!

BALIN. You are quite utterly contradictory.

BONDWOMAN. I have been turned inside-out and upside-down for the whole of my life – what else do you expect?

MONK. Do you intend to come or do you not?

BALIN (to BONDWOMAN). You will wait?

BONDWOMAN. I don't know. I am the greed of deceitful Eve – you can't trust me.

> *She sits back on the bundle and continues to eat the apple.* BALIN *and the* MONK *go out.* MERLIN *suddenly comes sliding across to her.*

MERLIN. But you *can* trust me. Get out of this – quick! (*He has thrown back the hood of his cloak and she stares at him, wide-eyed.*)

BONDWOMAN. Oh my God, it's the Chief Poet! And I thought you were a beggarman!

MERLIN. Child, you are in great peril. Now you know me. I speak truth.

BONDWOMAN. I think that you do. (*She goes out rapidly.*)

MERLIN (*singing*).

That angel white and gold did sing
A dangerous tune to Pellam King.
The wind of it now blows my cloak
In such a curious way that it must bring
    With clattering wing
Across the hill and through the wood
The tattered dragon and his brood –
General, come down – I have made plain

The mystery that Pellam would have hid
... Rusted with blood.

While singing, he has taken off his cloak and waved it several times like a signal flag at the front of the stage, as though communicating with someone at a great distance. Then he pulls it once more over his shoulders.

And that will do very well for that. Now then, for a safe place to sit me down and wait for them. Not half-an-hour, I would imagine . . . 'Lord Jesus, a great revenge is coming upon you'. (*He leaves.*)

GARLON *re-enters. He is wearing a soldier's defensive coat and steel cap, and he drags the* BONDWOMAN *after him.*

GARLON. So I have got you again, damn my blood, but I will keep you!

BONDWOMAN. Ah no, I will not be dragged! If you want me you must ask for me. God knows I might say yes . . .

GARLON. You would say yes to any man that put a tight enough grip on you.

BONDWOMAN. Help, help, Balin – it's Garlon, help, he has me!

Running feet are heard from both sides of the stage. The first to enter are PELLAM *and the* MONK, *at opposite sides.*

PELLAM. What is this –? Here is brawling, and a bloodthirsty desecration. Take your hands off that woman!

GARLON *stands undecided.* BALIN *runs in, from the same side as the* MONK, *he leaps from behind onto* GARLON *and kills him with a chop of the edge of his hand.* BALIN *is unarmed.*

BALIN.
For fear of sacrilege, they said,
My two swords must be left aside.
With my bare hands I fought this devil dead
I broke the neckbone underneath his head!

PELLAM. You have killed –

MONK. At the very moment you were about to have revealed to you the Holy Relic –

PELLAM (*looking at* GARLON). He was my soldier. I recruited him this very morning. You come to my quiet house and straightaway

set about to commit manslaughter among my people! Where are
my guards! I will have you hanged. Within five minutes.

Two GUARDS *enter, dressed in the same gear as* GARLON. BALIN
*poises himself, ready to dodge as they advance upon him with their
swords out.*

BALIN.
    So catch me where I run.
    Let me but get my two good swords again –
    By God we shall have some fun.

The GUARDS *go for him, he evades and there is complete confusion for a short while as they all hunt him around, on and off the
stage and in and out of the wings. For an instant the stage is left
empty except for the* BONDWOMAN. MERLIN, *passing rapidly
across, bumps into her.*

MERLIN. I thought I told you to get out of it!

The chase comes back again onto the stage.

    Balin – Balin – this way, you young idiot –!
BONDWOMAN. Balin, Balin, stop –!

She runs out after BALIN. *Then he comes back, without her. This
time he is cornered. He is holding a long black Spear.*

BALIN.
    I don't know what they have done with my two swords.
    Worm-eaten indeed, but it will serve.
    I'll teach that holy rascal to go calling for his guards.

    MERLIN *re-enters, sees what is happening, and stops short.*
MERLIN. No, you fool – no – not with that one! No!
BALIN. They kept it in a sort of a back kitchen cupboard, all sur-
    rounded with burning candles –
MERLIN. It might even be what they claim it to be –
BALIN. So what if it is?

The GUARDS, *in awe of the Spear, have kept their distance, but
they are cutting off his retreat.* PELLAM *re-enters.*

MERLIN.
    Pellam, stand still!
    Don't you see – he has your Spear!

PELLAM (*advancing upon* BALIN *in horror*).
　　Sacrilege – the curse of God –
　　God strike you down – sacrilege.
BALIN.
　　He said stand still!
　　Do you think I do not dare?
　　Do you think I have not the will?
　　Then continue so to think
　　For as long as your eyes can blink.
　　He runs PELLAM *through. The Spear breaks.* PELLAM *falls in a*
　　tangle with his toga, the sharp end of the Spear stuck into his
　　thighs. BALIN *is left standing, the shaft in his hand.*
PELLAM. Sacrilege, sacrilege, it was the Spear of Jesus Christ.
　　A great noise offstage – thunder and lighting, shouting, the crash of
　　horse-hooves and the blare of trumpets, etc.

SCENE SIX

Raid.

BEDWYR *and* COMPANIONS *enter suddenly from all sides.* BEDWYR
carries the dragon-standard and they all are in their war-gear with
their naked weapons in their hands.

They charge forward and strike down PELLAM's GUARDS. *The*
MONK *comes running in and falls on his knees when he sees what is*
happening. The BONDWOMAN *runs in from the other side, is caught*
up in a fight between a COMPANION *and one of the* GUARDS *– she*
runs screaming. BALIN *gets hold of her and tries to take her safely*
away, but in the swirl of soldiery they are separated and go out at
different sides of the stage. The BONDWOMAN *can be heard screaming*
offstage.

The whole scene is lit by the glare of flames. The noise and confusion
lasts a very short time. As silence falls, ARTHUR *enters at the back. He*
walks downstage, very much in command of himself and everyone else,
leaning on his stick. He is in civilian clothes, with riding boots.

ARTHUR. And that, by the looks of it, will do very well for that.
　　Sound the recall.

BEDWYR. *Bucinator, revocationem sona.*

ARTHUR. Form the men into their ranks – we stay here no longer than we have to – we must be on the road again for Carlisle without one moment's hesitation.

BEDWYR. *Ordine signum sequere praeparate.*

The COMPANIONS *disperse.*

ARTHUR. Has everything been done that I ordered to be done?

BEDWYR. Every one of Pellam's people that we found here has been killed, we have set fire to his house and his barracks and all his fortifications. Not a moment of resistance. We took him entirely by surprise.

ARTHUR. Pellam himself?

BEDWYR (*pointing to* PELLAM). He's not dead, but he's –

PELLAM. Incurable!

ARTHUR. Done for. His camp of treachery concluded, my lines of communication safe.

One of the COMPANIONS *re-enters with a golden diadem in his hand.*

COMPANION. We found this. He must have had it made. It's a kind of crown, I think.

ARTHUR. Dear God, it is the Diadem of Imperial Rome, would you credit it! Yet the man deserves some pity. His Roman ancestors owned all these lands and more. With their slaves and great granaries and their trading ships upon the sea –

PELLAM. To Spain, Italy, Egypt – they sent cargoes and laid out money. They had letters-of-credit drawn upon commercial houses in both Rome and Alexandria. They could correspond with the Emperor and their advice would be acted upon –

ARTHUR. And all for their own enrichment and the oppression of their people. Which is not the sort of Empire that I choose to remember. Rather justice, restraint of power, protection for the weak. I have laid waste your little kingdom, I might as well spare your life. Oh yes . . . there is a Spear you have been intoning great psalms about. Where is it?

PELLAM. Incurable . . . !

ARTHUR (*seeing the Spear in* PELLAM's *body*). Ah . . . we will leave it where it is. Let this barefoot beard who put the nonsense in your mind pull the steel out of your flesh – if he is able. We go

ARTHUR. *Signum proferite.*

BEDWYR. *Signum prolatum est, duce. Ad equius, suberite prae-parate.*

> ARTHUR *and his men all go out. The* MONK, *weeping loudly, drags* PELLAM *away.* BALIN *re-enters. In his arms he carries the* BONDWOMAN, *dead.* MERLIN *re-enters, holding* BALIN's *two swords.*

BALIN. I found her lying dead just outside the boundary of the house. There was a stream at the bottom of a green slope and she lay with her head in the water.

MERLIN. You struck one blow –

BALIN. But not against her –

MERLIN.

> Yes indeed, you struck one blow.
> You did not think, you did not know
> What it was you meant to do.
> When Pellam stood before you
> He held neither spear nor sword
> He was a poor defeated deluded lord –

BALIN.

> He had called for his guard –

MERLIN.

> And you had full time to look at his poverty
> And you had full time to extend to him your charity–
> For you and for other men who are burdened with no authority
> To authorize your own strength 'is' your highest oppor-tunity –

Do you not think my General would be glad so to have it! I suppose she was hit on the head by the hooves of one of the great war-horses. In the confusion of the attack, when they all ran this way and that . . .

Let me take her – I will bury her.

BALIN.

> I had thought that I might marry her.

MERLIN.

> Except that she was a slave.

BALIN.

> Yet nonetheless she gave

Some words to me that might have changed it –
'Make friends with Garlon,' she said.
And I broke his neck beneath his head.
Do you think it could have been
The old blood upon the Spear that so arranged it,
Marking each one of us with a cross of rusted red?
I believe that I too had a blow upon the head . . .

He lays the body down upon the ground, not far from GARLON's.

MERLIN.
When the horsemen came charging
They don't care where they ride –
It is their nature and their trade –
And I waved them down the hill
To follow it through.

BALIN.
Tell me now – where shall I go?
Tell me – what shall I do?
These swords belong to me.
Stick to my hand.
This spear-shaft, I laid hold of it.
Stick to my hand.

He has had the shaft of the Spear held under his elbow all this time. He now holds it in one hand. With the other hand he takes both his swords from MERLIN. *He holds all these weapons out in front of him and looks at them dazedly.*

MERLIN.
So many weapons and not one day of good fortune.

BALIN. I saw some small fishing boats pulled up over there on a
sandbank of the estuary. There is a wind towards Ireland. I can
manage a boat myself; my father taught me. If I go to Ireland, no
one will ever know that I was once a nobleman.
They might make me a slave.
She would smile if she heard of that
And take a bite out of her sour apple
If she's able to move her elbows
In her dark narrow grave.

Exit BALIN.

MERLIN.

> The wind blows to the west
> And it scratches the salt scalp of the wave.
> *Sings.*
> On wild Balin I have put all
> The blame and burden of this deed,
> And let him go, half-lunatic,
> Clutching his guilty weapons to his side,
>   Swift on the tide.
>
> To Ireland can he carry off
> The murder that I helped to do?
> My General gave me his commands.
> I did obey, it was my trade, I knew
> The truth – did you?
>
> The only truth this child could know
> From all the men who ever used her
> Was truth of Garlon's rage and fear –
> This bandit told her true. He did abuse her.
> Oh yet he loved her.

What word apart from his foul word
Can now be trusted in these days?
I am the General's Poet – I make
The words that make him famous in his age –
> War must he wage
> Poetry must praise
> Such war until he wins
> How can he ever win
> Without blemish of sin?
> Dead men are carried in
> Praise the death and the killing
> My words are ever willing
> In the service of his sword –
> Oh my merciful Lord
> It was not me who called
> The hard horse-hoof
> Upon this tender head
> Stark dead!

He goes out, carrying the body of the BONDWOMAN.

SCENE SEVEN

Fort.

BEDWYR *and* COMPANIONS *enter briskly and remove dead bodies or anything else left over from previous scene. Then they go out again.*

Enter ARTHUR *and* MEDRAUT (*in civilian clothes, both of them*), STRATHCLYDE, *with his arm in a sling, and* TALIESIN.

MEDRAUT. But you confected the whole bad business without one word to me of what you were planning! My brother Strathclyde in all innocence marched off to his own defeat and now we discover that your only purpose in permitting it was the deception and destruction of Pellam!

ARTHUR. I have explained it was necessary. My lines of communication to the fortresses in the south –

MEDRAUT. Were under threat. So very good. So whose Christian land do we go and lay waste next?

STRATHCLYDE. Mine!

MEDRAUT. And no doubt I won't be told of it. You don't appear to realize, uncle, that my honour is involved in this. It was me who passed on your solemn promises to Strathclyde –

TALIESIN. I warned my lord about those promises. I told him that the General never regarded the Picts as a serious danger at all!

ARTHUR. The General was quite right. Consider it in all coolness – if such a condition is possible to your confused and roaring minds – you have *not* been invaded by the People of the Wild Cat. Well, have you? So very good. Medraut, you are my Lieutenant. Your honour? You have no honour. It is the honour of the entire Army and you can leave me to take care of it.

MEDRAUT. But –

ARTHUR. So very good. I am now in a position to take my proper defensive steps against the onslaught of the English heathen. Defence, as we term it, in depth. The land of Strathclyde is my base. The land of Gododdin on the north-east coast is where I put forward my outposts. If you attempt to interfere with my headquarters in Carlisle, or with my lines of communication, you will be served the same as Pellam. Make no mistake about that; you are one of the hereditary rulers whom we are bound to defend, and defended you will be, though it cost you your life and your crown and every acre you possess. There's a paradox. Here's another one: young Medraut is supposed to be the leg upon which I do not limp – (ARTHUR, *in his excitement, has stumbled and nearly fallen.*) – now he's failing in his duty. Support me boy, why don't you, I have a parade-ground to traverse!

He drags himself out, supported by MEDRAUT.

STRATHCLYDE. Oh yes, we can all hobble. Nothing left in Britain but a bloody pack of crippled blunderers . . . (*Exit*)

Enter MERLIN.

MERLIN. Taliesin Chief Poet.

TALIESIN. I hold you more to blame than anyone else.

MERLIN. Oh yes, I daresay. That girl you once provided me – you know who I mean – how did she come to be your personal bond-servant?

TALIESIN. She had a brother who was my pupil, about ten years ago. He stole a very valuable book from me and eloped. I demanded the price of the book from his father, who was of course unable to pay. He was some sort of small-holder, there were poets in his family, but neither gold nor silver. So I took the girl. She was a bad bargain. A thief and a runaway just like her brother.

MERLIN. I have heard she is dead.

TALIESIN. Not surprised at it at all. Fit consequence of her immorality.
    Fit consequence of your General's behaviour
    If he too comes to his death.

MERLIN.
    You have noticed no doubt
    He is very short of breath.
    When he moves, it is with pain.
    He is now setting out
    Upon his last great campaign
    I will help him to gain the victory
    Though it cost me my life
    And my truth and my poetic integrity.

TALIESIN. Which is as much as to say you have considerable mis-
 givings.
MERLIN. Ah yes, but about what?
TALIESIN. For my part, I think that your General has gone mad.
 (*Exit*)
MERLIN.
  I do not want to bother any more
  With Balin and with Balan.
  If you're interested to hear what happened
  Let him tell you who best can . . .

  MERLIN *leaves. As he goes out – and crossing his movement – the*
  PICTISH POET *comes in, and takes up* MERLIN's *usual place on
  the forestage.*

PICTISH POET (*singing*).
  There was a young man and to Ireland he did sail
  For he thought the wind was fair.
  But it blew him to the south and it blew him to the north
  And it blew him to the Galloway shore.

SCENE EIGHT

Seascape.

PICTISH POET (*continues singing*).
  And when he came to the Galloway shore
  His boat was broke in three.
  In the strangle of the waves he was thrown overboard
  And they found him by the edge of the sea.

  BALIN, *still clutching his weapons, and soaked to the skin,
  staggers on to the stage and collapses.*

  There were two fishermen and the wife that they had
  And they did not know what to do
  With a half-drowned man who had a scar upon his face
  And not one sword but two.

  The two FISHERMEN *and their* WIFE *have come in and are
  examining* BALIN *with alarm and great circumspection.*

Seascape

FIRST FISHERMAN. It is himself of whom our Poet warned us, that
is for certain.

SECOND FISHERMAN. And what is this he still holds in his cold
hand – the broken butt of an old spear?

FIRST FISHERMAN. Maybe it is all that he had to steer his boat
with. He was little use at the management of it, whatever.

FISHERMEN'S WIFE. The Old Lady must be told of this.

FIRST FISHERMAN. Is that needful? We could rummage through
his sporran and take whatever he has and then throw him back
into the sea.

SECOND FISHERMAN. And no one need know he had come here.
Myself I am in fear to go to the Old Lady. There is likely to be

some defilement upon us for any meddling with such matters and
then it will cost us months of purgative diet and maybe abstention
from the bed of this woman until we are held to be clean.

FISHERMEN'S WIFE. You must at all events be made clean. You are
defiled already. You have touched him. Do not you forget he is
said to have murdered –

FIRST FISHERMAN. We know that too well. We are in fear of it.

FISHERMEN'S WIFE. It seems to me you are in fear of everything,
the pair of you. I tell you this – neither love from my body nor
food from my hand shall you have until our Queen has been
informed.

SECOND FISHERMAN. Then tell her yourself, woman, when you go
to take up the basket of fish for the Goddess. It would be better
after all if the word of it came from you.

FIRST FISHERMAN. From a devout woman – oh much better.

FISHERMEN'S WIFE. There is no need. The Queen is here.

SECOND FISHERMAN. Has she come down all by herself to collect
her own fish?

FIRST FISHERMAN. Not usual. I don't like it.

SECOND FISHERMAN. I don't care for it indeed.

Enter the QUEEN, *followed at a little distance by her* WAR-
LEADER *and two* GIRLS, *in attendance.*
The QUEEN *looks carefully at* BALIN.

POET (*singing*).
Our wise old Queen has a magic looking-glass
She holds it in her withered hand
And therein she espies every uncouth thing
That happens through the length of her land.

QUEEN. Is he drowned then, did you discover?

FISHERMEN'S WIFE. There is yet breath in him, but not much.

POET (*singing*).
Of the royal men and women of the Wild Cat Tribe
Not one of them knew what to do.
Should we kill him where he lies or revive him back to life
That the Goddess should receive her due?

QUEEN. Two swords, and one of them belongs to me. But what is
this shaft of a spear?

BALIN (*sitting up, half in a trance*).
Ran into the side of Jesus

Blood and water trickled down it
No good luck is left upon it.

POET (*he has gone over to join the* QUEEN *and her retinue*). The last man that came to us was a man of no good luck. Or so he said.

WAR-LEADER. He also said he had committed no crime.

QUEEN. Oh, this one has committed a crime and we know well what it is.

POET. But since the last man walked upon the island for us, both him and the whole people have prospered as never before.

FIRST GIRL. The youngest granddaughter of the Queen has already proved with child.

FISHERMEN'S WIFE. There is a glut of silver fish.

SECOND GIRL. The crop of oats from the field above the glen is whiter and heavier than it has been for seven years.

WAR-LEADER. You are certain the King did all that? Maybe . . . I will add one other benefit – no more intruding Christians have put foot across our boundary because if they did, I made an end of them. Oh, I don't claim any credit for the clemency of the weather.

There is a pause. The QUEEN *goes over to the* FISHERMEN's *basket and starts examining the fish.*

BALIN.
Make an end then, make an end.
So far from sight of land.
So wild a storm upon the water
Ropes break, ribs crack,
Sail and oars are scattered –
Bitter salt fills up my mouth
Spit it out with a great oath –
Make an end, make an end!
I have given my bad hand
To the work of so much slaughter.

POET. Jesus. He was a God and a King. His Mother was the Star of the Sea, and when we travel in our fishing boats that is also the title that we put upon our own Mother.

QUEEN. True . . .

POET. He died in Her service, as our own God and King every year must face death in *your* service, upon the island.

QUEEN. True . . .

POET. But here is where the mistake lies. The Roman conquerors stole Him from us. He belonged to all men, and in particular to men like ourselves who have a true veneration for His Blessed and Most Terrible Mother.

QUEEN. Such men in such times are of necessity poor and hungry.

BALIN.

> Poor men and hungry.
> I did not know why they were so angry
> So angry that their thoughts run thick and mirk
> And every blow they strike must miss its mark.
> Salt water in my mouth.
> I vomit out with a great oath:
> For such good men that their bellies may be full
> I strike my blows alone and strike them with good will.
> I am no more a nobleman.
> I am quite other and out of the law.
> Garlon I have been
> And Barabbas and branded Cain.
> Direct will be my hand.
> Clear will be my brain.

WAR-LEADER. No great clearness in it yet, at all events. Nor in all this talk about Jesus whatever. This man is not Jesus, he is a Christian Roman and I think we should cut his throat.

POET. We?

WAR-LEADER. I myself, if it comes to that.

QUEEN. No, not yourself. Here is too strange a work for you, old soldier.

> This man has been sent to us
> At this very particular time.
> He has certain words and a certain Spear
> And his very particular crime.
> He also has his brother.
> Can we change one for the other?

POET.

> Bad luck or good luck?

FIRST GIRL.

> Would we lose or would we gain?

SECOND GIRL.

> Consider the two of them.
> They are exactly the same.

POET.
Except that this one has the Spear.

WAR-LEADER. Now look – we are in grave danger of peering far too deeply into what has been seen in a magic mirror, but in my opinion should remain hid. There is a correct time of the year for this business upon the island, and I tell you it is not now. Old lady, I am nearly as old as you, I am too old to be intimidated. Take the gifts the Goddess has granted us and be content with what we have.

The QUEEN, *who until now has been quietly peering in her mirror, suddenly begins to rattle in her throat and goes into a rigid posture – a medium entering a trance.*

POET (*to* WAR-LEADER). Ah yes, you may well turn as white as a fish-belly. She will now speak with the tongue of the Goddess, and who knows at her age she is not going to die of it?

The QUEEN *continues with her uncouth noises, and the* POET *interprets them into speech. As he does so he performs a kind of jerking dance all around the stage. The* GIRLS *clap their hands to the strongly-marked rhythm.*

POET (*chanting*).
Into the boat and then
Out of the boat and so
Onto the shore
So let him walk on the
Island no sword in his
Hand but the Spear
Meet with his brother the
Other my hand shall my
Judgement declare
By hand of the victor oh
Which of the pair of them
I hold most dear.

She finishes and collapses, her breath coming in great gulps. The GIRLS *tend her.*

The Goddess has spoken. She will soon be herself again . . . Dress him and garland him and make him drunk for the conflict. He is half-way in a trance already; the delirium of the Goddess is

churning in his bowels as well as in hers. Old soldier; are you
subdued . . . ?

> *Exeunt all but the* POET – BALIN *goes out supported by the*
> FISHERMEN, *while the* QUEEN *is helped by her* GIRLS.

SCENE NINE

Woodland.

Enter BALAN *and the* PRINCESS, *arm-in-arm. He limps, being now
lame in the left foot. They sit down and he sprawls indolently in her lap.*

POET (*singing*).
　　All under the leaves and the leaves of gold
　　He lies with his golden love
　　The sword with which he won her is corroded and old
　　And forgotten is the death that it drove.

　　He suddenly shouts in a tremendous voice.

　If you don't kill him, he will kill you!

BALAN *and the* PRINCESS *leap to their feet in terror.*

BALAN. But you told me I would have a year and a day, undisturbed, before the challenge!

PRINCESS. It has always been the custom, so. I don't understand
what's happened.

BALAN (*staggering about helplessly*).
　　I am all fat and bloated
　　I think my brains have floated
　　All these weeks in a cup of your vile liquor
　　I have rolled naked without control
　　Upon every maiden and grown girl
　　Who uncovered her breast and her thighs
　　For the delight of my bloodshot eyes –
　　The lake, the whole island are swaying all around me –
　　How can I defend me –?
　　When I came here you told me

I would fight for you and be free.
Is this your Wild Cat liberty
To have me halt on a leg and a half?
Your Goddess is a great tossing cow
Who runs her mortal horn
Into the eyeball of her own calf
And then drops her stinking dung
All over the milkmaid's pail –

The POET *fetches* BALAN's *white cat-mask and the bronze sword
and hands them to the* PRINCESS. *She holds them out to* BALAN.

No, I won't put it on!
PRINCESS.
      I swear it will protect you –
      I swear you will prevail –
BALAN.
      If I do I will come back to you
      I will carve up your lovely udders
      And cut off your treacherous tail.

*She forces the mask down over his head and puts the sword into his
hand.* BALIN *comes in, wearing the big black cat-mask, and holding the butt of the Spear.*

BALIN (*to himself*).
      I seem to be set forward
      To meet some enemy and to fight.
      I have had no provocation,
      Been given no information
      Which one of us wrong
      And which one of us is right.
      I took an oath: I am prohibited.
      I will keep well away from him
      And hold my sword upside-down –
      No, it isn't a sword –
      I don't know what it is – what –?
      I cannot possibly fight a man
      Who is dressed up like a clown . . .
Moreover he is a cripple and it would be dishonourable to take
advantage. I am not without honour, though I am no longer a
nobleman.

BALAN (*to himself*). Comes against me with nothing but a splintered
bit of wood. I do believe he is afraid of me! (*He laughs. Then calls
across to* BALIN.) I do believe you are afraid of me!

BALIN (*to himself*). He should not say that. He is going to make me
angry. I will forget my prohibition. (*Calls across to* BALAN.)
You should not have said that! (*To himself again.*) By God if
I am laughed at I will forget everything I have learnt. I
am not very old and my father is dead; all these prohibitions
are too difficult for me to deal with. (*Across to* BALAN *again.*)
Look you here – I am a nobleman and I will prove it with my
sword!

POET.
If you do not kill him, he will kill you!

> Spurred on by the POET's shout, they run at each other violently.
> BALIN drives his splintered wood into BALAN's groin and BALAN
> shortens his sword and chops lethally into BALIN's breast.
> They both lie on the ground. The PRINCESS throws herself upon
> BALAN with uncontrollable sobs.
> He pulls off his mask with great difficulty and sits up and looks at
> BALIN. He laughs – a very painful laugh – and feebly pushes the
> PRINCESS off him so that he can get a better view of BALIN.

BALIN.
By God we are both dead.
Your head and my head
Are now jangling bang bang bang
Upon the necklace of this foolish Goddess.
I hear her weeping – she is in distress.
Not credible she should weep
For the man she helped to murder.
Ah yes, she has now no lover
No cocked-up King to roll and stumble
From end to end of her bed.
Uncover his head.
Let me see the little fellow
I have laid him so still and dead.

> The POET goes over to BALIN and lifts off the mask. BALAN
> recognizes his brother and laughs. BALIN slowly opens his eyes and
> recognizes BALAN.

Oh why oh why did you ever say good bye
Without shaking my hand?
Give it me if you can.

BALIN *crawls over and holds out his hand.*

BALIN.
Take it and shake it and never let go of it.
I don't understand anything that has happened or where I am or what . . . ?
BALAN.
Oh dear brother you never understood
One single thing you ever did.
BALIN. How did you come to be crippled in your left leg?
BALAN. These people have ill customs. (*He dies.*)
POET. We make our King lame so that he cannot escape. And then after all his pleasuring the next King finds it easy to kill him. Until now the custom was good. But certain of our people came to believe it should be put an end to, and I think that that is what the Goddess has now done. Whether or no we turn Christian as a result of it, is a matter to be considered.

Enter the QUEEN.

QUEEN.
You will *not* consider that.
Until my day has come
For the Goddess to take me home.
Oh savage Lady of the Glen
Come soon come soon, O come for me soon . . .
BALIN.
I think it is the Roman horsemen
Who will come to trample you down.
But I saw them, they are such old men
Strapped up with hooks of iron.
It should not be at all impossible
For you to knock them out of their saddles –
And then you yourselves – you –
Can you grip hold of their strong bridles?

BALIN *dies.*

PRINCESS.

> The King is dead, we have no King no more
> No food no love but only hopeless war.
> How can we think we can win it
> When we don't know who we are?

The POET *returns to the forestage.*
QUEEN *and* PRINCESS *exeunt.* BEDWYR (*carrying dragon-standard*) *and* COMPANIONS *enter, in war-gear. They hastily drag off the corpses, etc., and then re-enter.* MERLIN *enters in his official dress.*

POET (*singing*).

> Old men old men on their horses so huge
> And their dragon so high on its pole
> They never will believe that for them there is a grave
> Just as deep as for those whom they kill.

MERLIN. Oh no, my heathen friend – not true. We are only too well aware of the depth of our graves.

The PICTISH POET *bows gravely to him and goes out.*

SCENE TEN

Camp.

Enter ARTHUR *and* MEDRAUT *in their war-gear.* ARTHUR *speaks directly to the audience.*

ARTHUR. Companions: for thirty years I have commanded you and for thirty years you have obeyed me without question. You have recognized my authority as the only representative of what was once the Roman Empire. My father Uther was Chief Dragon General – before him there was his brother Ambrosius Aurelian – and they were the heroic grandsons of the General Magnus Maximus who had been appointed to the command of the troops of the entire Island by Gratianus Caesar who sat on the throne of Rome. Magnus Maximus was a Roman, he married the daughter of an hereditary Prince of Britain, he was the first who set up the

Red Dragon as the emblem of his Army, he brought the Dragon and his British soldiers across the water into Gaul, and out of Gaul into Italy, and he took hold of Gratianus, that dull and cowardly ruler, and he cut off his head. Magnus Maximus from that day forth became sole Emperor of the Western World. In due time he was defeated, but his victories had been his own, and the sword with which he won them now hangs here at my belt. (*He draws his long cavalry sword and holds it proudly in front of him.*) Such is my authority but, had I been dull and cowardly, had I not proved my generalship in twelve great battles without faint-heartedness, then you would have had no reason to obey me, and I would have had not a single show of pretext for demanding your obedience. Yet I do demand it. I demand it confidently: I know I will not be deceived. We are all of us now confronted with the most dangerous invasion our people have endured since Hengist and Horsa first brought their wicked ships into the estuary of Thames. I have this day heard the news – an enormous force of English has come ashore upon the north-east coast. I have had to withdraw my outposts inland twenty or thirty miles – so heavily are we outnumbered. I have sent messengers to Caerleon for the rest of the Army to ride north. When they get here, they will be deployed with yourselves in a general campaign that is likely to last throughout the winter. The weather will be bad. Your work will be difficult. The enemy is most ferocious. We will fight against him ruthlessly, we will defeat him without mercy. In the Name of Christ, let me remind you, we are not predestined to win. Too much pride in our past glory may lead us toward carelessness, lack of discipline, foolhardiness, disorder, and the destruction of all that we stand for. Companions: you alone are responsible for the continued religion and civilization of Britain. This Island has been called by her poets 'The Island of the Mighty'. Do not betray that title.

Exeunt

THE ISLAND
OF THE MIGHTY

Part Two

'OH, THE CRUEL WINTER'

Concerning Arthur –
how he refused to see that
the power of his army
was finished

SCENE ONE

Woodland.

Enter MERLIN, TALIESIN *and* CHIEF POETS, *all in their official dress. They group themselves in a semi-circle and sit down.*

MERLIN (*singing*).
> The Chief Poets of Britain come together among the trees
> Like trees in the winter wind I hear their old bones creak
> Bones and brains complain, rheumatism in head and in knee
> There are times I think it a wonder such a congregation should
>> include me.
> Taliesin is the most venerable, therefore he is the first to speak.

TALIESIN. No maker of verse in the Island of Britain is permitted to describe himself as Chief Poet unless and until a properly-constituted College of Bards has adjudicated his claim. We have such a claimant come before us today. Who sponsors him?

FIRST CHIEF POET. I do.

TALIESIN. Very good.

FIRST CHIEF POET. His name is Aneurin. He was my pupil for ten years. And afterward, he tells me, he has followed his craft at the court of the Prince of Gododdin, in Dunedin, upon the Firth of Forth. As a student, he gave me great hope. I do not know what he has done since.

TALIESIN. Very good. Let him be called for.

FIRST CHIEF POET Aneurin Poet, you may set yourself forward before the College of Bards.

ANEURIN (*entering*). Good morning.

MERLIN (*singing*).
> His appearance is bad: his manner inclines to be rude
> Unless his verse is the verse of a very Virgil I think he will not
>> be approved.

TALIESIN. Aneurin Poet, a theme has been given you by this College for the construction of an Ode in a specified metre. You have completed the poem?

ANEURIN. Oh yes.

TALIESIN. Then let us hear it, and we may pass judgment upon your ability. First give a summary of the theme and afterward recite the verses.

ANEURIN. The Burial of the Head of Bran the Blessed, ancestor of all the royal houses of the Island of the Mighty. In the days before the Romans came, this great hero died in battle and his head was laid separately to rest upon the bank of the River Thames. We are told that so long as it remains there, beneath its cairn of stones, no invader can successfully cross the grey sea and take possession of this Island. We are told so, and we all believe it. Nevertheless, the Romans came.

TALIESIN. What?

SECOND CHIEF POET. You were asked to state the given theme, not to dispute it.

MERLIN. If he wants to dispute it, he can do so in his verse. Let him continue.

TALIESIN. Before he continues, Merlin, I insist upon pointing out the lack of logic in his argument. The Romans did indeed come, and for four hundred years they stayed here. They intermingled with our people, they gave us government, built stone roads, and fortified towns, they provided us with the inestimable blessing of the Gospel of Christ. Not at all the sort of invasion against which we are defended by the Buried Skull of Bran. You of all men, Merlin, should be the first to agree with me.

MERLIN. I do. I do. I want to hear his poem.

TALIESIN. I am by no means sure that I do. At a time like this, moreover, when we are threatened on every side by the real deadly heathen – English and Saxons, in particular the abominable Picts –

ANEURIN. If you don't want me to recite, I will go.

MERLIN. You will not. You will show forth your quality. Begin now, if you please.

ANEURIN (*singing*).

> I was a wicked man
> And I had a wicked wife
> I could not endure her
> To live her wicked life.
> I could not endure her
> Not yet could I leave her
> Whatever she said to me
> I did not dare believe her –

TALIESIN. Enough – quite enough!

ANEURIN. Oh no, it's not, that's only the first stanza. You've not even heard the refrain – (*He sings.*)

> Oh the cruel winter
> And the pain of its arrival
> Young wives who will behave themselves
> Have small chance of survival . . .

FIRST CHIEF POET. I must offer my deepest apologies to the College of Bards. I cannot think what has happened to this young man. It is perfectly outrageous.

THIRD CHIEF POET. I am amazed that Gododdin should have thought fit to employ you. His father would never have tolerated such blackguardism at his court.

TALIESIN. Your candidature to the title of Chief Poet is disallowed. A few hundred years ago you could have been burnt alive for this.

Exeunt all except MERLIN *and* ANEURIN.

ANEURIN. For what?

MERLIN. You have insulted the Sacred College. Do I really need to explain to you? You ignored the specified metre which was Heroic. Instead you produced some low class of Satirical Ballad. You ignored the specified theme –

ANEURIN. I did not.

MERLIN. The Head of Bran the Blessed –

ANEURIN. Buried in the foundation of the bedroom of his house so that he could keep a continual eye upon the behaviour of his libidinous widow. If you had only bothered to listen to it you would have found out how it went on.

MERLIN. Not the traditional story, my young friend, and it's no good pretending it is.

ANEURIN. College of Bards –!

MERLIN. The Prince of Gododdin enjoys your impertinence, does he?

ANEURIN. The Prince of Gododdin makes use of me to write his letters and to add up his money. In my verse he has no interest.

MERLIN. Then for whom do you compose it?

ANEURIN. He has a widowed sister, the lady Gwenhwyvar. Wicked, she is, with eyes like green gooseberries.

MERLIN. And it was she who encouraged you to apply for the title of Chief Poet?

ANEURIN. Indeed not. It was Gododdin. He thought it would give his principality prestige. God knows it is in need of it.

MERLIN. It appears to me altogether you are not happy in your work.

ANEURIN. Are you? For whom do you compose?

MERLIN. For my master the General Chief Dragon.

ANEURIN. Does he listen?

MERLIN. I thought there might be some small ebb-and-flow of something agreeable in you, but there is not. You live like this all your life, you ingratiate yourself with nobody, nobody! Whatever possessed you, you should choose to become a poet?

ANEURIN. I made up a song once and I sang it to a travelling tinker. His eyes lighted up and he laughed at it and he *learnt* it. (*He sings.*)

> John Baptist out of the desert walked
> And all he wore was a cloth of hair –

MERLIN. Good God, you wrote that!

ANEURIN. You have heard it?

MERLIN. Upon the lips of a most violent murderer. A bandit of the wild wood. He used it to justify the enormity of his life.

ANEURIN. So the tinker must have repeated it. So it is in circulation, so it is! Do you know, that without knowing it, I might already be a famous man?

MERLIN. The man who sang it to me had never heard your name.

ANEURIN. Not important. Aha, he had heard my song!

Exit.

MERLIN (*singing*).

> So many have heard the songs
> I have made about Arthur my General
> So many more will remember them and remember my name
>   when I am dead.
> His own name will not be forgotten, he is aware of it as he lurks
>   in his tent
> As he crouches beneath his banner and looks up at the naked
>   head –

SCENE TWO

Camp.

ARTHUR *enters, dragging himself wearily across the stage. He is wearing his war-gear, and he carries the dragon-standard which he sets up at the side of the stage.*

MERLIN (*continues singing*).
Arthur, protector of Britain, himself protected, so it is said,
By this white globe of bone that once lay under the bank of Thames.

ARTHUR (*chanting rather than singing*).
It is the Head of Bran. I dug it up:
the charm has been brought to an end.
No magic now defends this Island, only the courage of me and my men.
We are mightier than Bran ever was, we endure a long living death
In the cold drag of the coming winter the English come onto us again and again —!

Where is my nephew Medraut? I sent him on patrol towards the sea coast to find out what he could find, he is a very great while about the business, do you think they've finished him?

MERLIN. He will come soon, I have no doubt.

ARTHUR. Merlin, you were with me, the night that I dug it up: you lifted the stones of the cairn and lifted out what had been put underneath them. It was a dark night and nobody saw what I did. Do you remember what I said?

MERLIN. You said that you would nail the skull to the crossbar of your battle-standard so that all your soldiers would know that a dead man is but dead: it takes a living man to lift him up.

ARTHUR. How could they know unless I told them what I had done? I intended to tell everyone, make a great declaration: but in the end it was kept secret, from all except yourself.

MERLIN. I have never spoken a word of it.

ARTHUR. Do you think that I should have? You see, *I* am aware that I have resisted superstition. Britain is not protected by the

head of an ancient hero turned into a discredited god. It is protected by an experienced Army under orders of a careful and
Christian General, who alone among his countrymen has read
books full of good sense. Titus Livius, Julius Caesar – when I was
young you could still lay hands on them and learn how to put
them together, word upon word, chapter upon chapter. I cut my
hair short, I turned myself back into a cool-headed Roman. But
my Companions were not quite that: Bran the Blessed was their
ancestor. It came to me suddenly that were I to deprive them of
him I might well be letting leak the darkest blood of their courageous hearts. So in silence I put him up, as a message to myself
alone. The Army no doubt believe he is the head of some Saxon or
other whom I killed – it is a trophy, nothing more. For them Bran
is still buried, and being buried is still alive. The more so that
with me they have won so many victories. (*He chants.*)

> And yet after all these years we stand and confront the cold
> winter
> The hungry English tug their oars and on our strand their keels
> come running in.
> Had I left him in the ground would they have left us alone do
> you think?
> What has happened to Medraut?
> I called that young man the leg on which I do not limp –
> I am too old to continue the campaign by myself
> if he should have been killed.

MERLIN (*changing*).

> Chief Dragon, he is alive, he is in the camp he has his music –
> hear it ring –

ARTHUR (*chanting*).

> I do not believe it will be good news he is bringing me . . .

With a flourish of music, MEDRAUT *and* COMPANIONS *enter in
their war-gear.*

MEDRAUT. I have examined the fortifications that the heathens have
erected.

ARTHUR. Yes?

MEDRAUT. Considering how little time they have had for it since
they came out of their ships, the work has been remarkably
thorough. Up to five miles inland from their landing place, a
complete group of stockades, trimmed and regular timber above

properly-scarped ditches, the whole affair made to a much better standard than anything I have ever heard of from the English before.

ARTHUR. Impregnable?

MEDRAUT. More or less.

ARTHUR. Call it impregnable. I am risking no soldiers in a rash and sudden attack.

MEDRAUT. God, no, I hope not.

ARTHUR. They are provisioned?

MEDRAUT. I saw one of their keels unloading barrels upon the beach.

ARTHUR. Dried and salted foodstuffs. They intend to stay here all the winter. I suppose they have no women and children with them?

MEDRAUT. Young men alone was all that I could see. Very formidable young men.

ARTHUR. This is the advanced party. They will take what land they can and hold it secure. And then, next year, in the good weather, they will bring the entire tribe over and we will never get rid of them. Did you see any horses?

MEDRAUT. No.

ARTHUR. Get them out of their stockades and drive on to them with the cavalry, we could destroy them all tomorrow.

MEDRAUT. But you won't get them out. I endeavoured it this afternoon. Ran around in front of their lines with a score of dismounted lancers and my music, taunting them, reviling them.

ARTHUR. It always worked before.

MEDRAUT. Oh, one of them came after me. And then he said he was a Flag-of-truce.

He flicks a gesture to the COMPANIONS, *two of whom go out and return at once with the* ENGLISHMAN, *blindfolded. The blindfold is taken off.*

Here he is. Calls himself a nobleman.

ARTHUR. Doesn't smell like a nobleman. He speaks our language, does he?

MEDRAUT. No. But I speak something of his.

ARTHUR. You do? Why was I not informed? You could be very useful with that.

MEDRAUT. Make use of me then.

ARTHUR. What does he want?

MEDRAUT. He has a letter 'for the enormous Worm' – I suppose he means the Chief Dragon. Oh, he has heard of you, yes.

ARTHUR. Letter? They don't write letters.

> MEDRAUT *has taken a dirty folded parchment from the belt of the* ENGLISHMAN *and passed it to* ARTHUR *who passes it to* MERLIN MERLIN *breaks the seal.*

MERLIN. It's not written in English.

MEDRAUT. Latin?

MERLIN. You won't believe it: but, yes.

ARTHUR. Merlin Chief Poet, who has written this letter, to whom is it addressed?

MERLIN. The grammar is extremely bad. It purports to be from the Prince of Gododdin to the war-leader of the English heathen – whose name is – I can't read it –

MEDRAUT (*to the* ENGLISHMAN). *Hwa het eower heretoga?*

ENGLISHMAN. *Ida Eoping* –

MEDRAUT. Ida, son of Eoppa.

ENGLISHMAN. *Eoppa wæs Esing, Esa Ingwiging, Ingwig Angen-witting, Angenwit Allocing* –

MEDRAUT. He is reciting the pedigree of his war-leader, do you want me to interpret?

ARTHUR. I do not. All I want to know is what and why has Gododdin been writing to these animals.

MERLIN. This letter gives permission for the war-bands of Ida to reside in the territories of Gododdin, provided that they keep to the less-populated areas and will fight for Gododdin when called upon to do so.

ARTHUR. I knew it. A Christian British Prince and he has *invited* them into his land!

MERLIN. There is no date upon the parchment.

ARTHUR. And what do you think *that* means?

MERLIN. It means it could be an invitation, or it could have been extorted by them after their arrival. I saw their behaviour here the first day that they came. If Gododdin was in fear of them he might very well send them this. I have reason to believe Gododdin is not competently advised. His so-called Chief Poet is –

MEDRAUT. Ungrammatical – you have told us.

MERLIN. Worse than that. I have met the man.

ARTHUR. Ask him when the letter was received.

MEDRAUT. *Hwonne brohte mon this ærendgewrit?*

ENGLISHMAN. *Aer thon the we of Seaxum foron.*

MEDRAUT. He says before they set sail from Germany, uncle.

ARTHUR. I don't believe it . . . but – oh yes, it could be true. Take him out.

MEDRAUT. Send him back?

ARTHUR. No. We'll hold him. Make him a hostage. And keep him blindfolded in the camp.

A COMPANION. *Iussa tua comprehendo et perficiam.*

COMPANIONS *blindfold the* ENGLISHMAN *and take him out.*

ARTHUR. I thought you said he did not understand any of our language.

MEDRAUT. No more he does.

ARTHUR. Every word of it, boy. Did you not see the crafty grin he gave when we talked about Gododdin, the look of outrage when I said he was to be kept here as a hostage? We will bear in mind his accomplishment and make use of it when we need to. I am more cheerful than I was. I have discovered two good linguists in the course of one short evening. It is possible our civilization does not lapse into complete savagery quite as rapidly as I feared.

With a gesture he dismisses the remaining COMPANIONS: *they go out.*

Nephew, what would you say if you were told that the Head of Bran the Blessed had been stolen from its resting-place?

MEDRAUT. I wouldn't say anything. I am a Christian. This is part of the old religion – it should not concern me –

ARTHUR. Good.

MEDRAUT. But I daresay I might think that our good luck would turn to bad.

ARTHUR. Supposing we had any good luck in the first place.

MEDRAUT. Yes.

ARTHUR. Not sufficient. Your education is not yet sufficient. Languages, they mean nothing. And you are the one to whom, in my absence, I must turn over the command of my whole Army, valiant Companions, grey-haired believers in the virtues of the Head of Bran.

MEDRAUT. Your absence? Where are you going?

ARTHUR. Dunedin. To confront this foolish Prince there and find out what he's been playing at. He must be persuaded to renounce his agreement with the English. He may be of no help to me in the war, but the danger of his example is incalculable in these times. No: I cannot send you. Too serious a business altogether to be left to subordinates. Merlin, you'll come with me, have a word with his Chief Poet.

MEDRAUT. And your orders for the Army, while you are gone?

ARTHUR. No. You tell me. Tell me what tactics you think best to be pursued.

MEDRAUT. I fancy you will not agree with them. However. He has his forts, he won't come out, we should have stopped him before he got them built, we were too late. It was an error. An error I attribute directly to the clumsiness of our organization. The heavy cavalry –

ARTHUR. The heavy cavalry was created by me as the only answer to the heathen onslaught. We hit hard and we move fast –

MEDRAUT. We used to move fast. We do not any longer. At the Battle of Badon – what – twenty years ago? – we took the South Saxons and the Kentish heathen completely by surprise. Uncle, we haven't done it this time. Therefore I suggest we let him stay where he is, shut in behind his fence. He can't get out. I occupy myself throughout the winter in recruiting. A new force altogether, quite different conception. Skirmishers, armed with bows-and-arrows, maybe javelins, mounted upon ponies. They'll need hardly any training. They already exist. The wild tribesmen of the hill districts – I can enlist them a whole clan at a time – put them under the command of their own accepted chiefs. Not a trooper of them shall be more than twenty-five years old, and I shall be their General.

ARTHUR. And what title do you propose to accord to this well-ordered regiment?

MEDRAUT. I think nothing Roman. I think it is too late for that. 'The Hounds of Bran', perhaps, to give them a sense of native inheritance. Ah no, you don't like it . . .

ARTHUR. Barbarous reversion to outmoded pagan futility! You talk about being too late! You are five hundred years too late! You cannot ignore the great Emperors and what they did.

MEDRAUT.

> They had big houses built
> And then they found
> That after they themselves
> Were laid beneath the ground
> Those men who with their own rough hands
> Had set the stones and trowelled the mortar in
> Preferred to let the sumptuous walls fall down –
> And now, in ditches and in trenches,
> The silly fellows are content
> To shelter under turf and branches.
> The old land-lord is dead and gone.
> At best you are his bastard son –
> What do you inherit
> That was not already your own?

ARTHUR. My – my –

MEDRAUT. Your title. You are the Emperor's deputy in the Island of Britain. Where is the Emperor?

ARTHUR. My – my –

MEDRAUT. Your sword. It belonged to Magnus Maximus. He conquered no further than Gaul.

ARTHUR. There is also my –

MEDRAUT. Army. And upon this occasion it has failed to take the enemy by surprise. So what do you propose to say to the Prince of Gododdin? He is a Sovereign Prince. We know it is unwise of him to let the English in. But who is to forbid it and according to what authority?

MERLIN. Chief Dragon, alas, your nephew is talking very good sense.

ARTHUR. If he were not I would have kicked his words out of his mouth. With my lame left foot I would have kicked them. I could compel Gododdin, deal with him as I dealt with Pellam, but not him and the English together. Besides, to do that always, every Prince who stands against me –

MERLIN. You would need to proclaim yourself Caesar Augustus of Britain and you would need to have done it at least twenty years ago.

ARTHUR. Some of my Companions once urged me that I should. I refused. I said I had no right to it. I said I was only the General. I was the servant, not the master.

MEDRAUT. Then be the servant: pay attention to the desires of your employer. He lives in a thatched hut, acknowledges no Emperor but the chief of his clan, and rides to the battle with gaiety upon the back of a long-tailed pony.

ARTHUR. Aha, you want your skirmishers! If you think it will work, I do not forbid it. But you are not to call yourself General. My Lieutenant. That is enough.

MEDRAUT. More than enough, uncle. I never believed you would even consider it.

ARTHUR. Gododdin is a man whose acquaintance I have not made. I did know his father. What has happened to the son? Merlin, we go and find out.

MEDRAUT. It is a long journey to Dunedin. Merlin, he is not in good health. Take care of him, for God's sake.

MERLIN. And do you take care of his Army with an equivalent diligence – I am sure we shall then have nothing to fear.

MEDRAUT. I should have some authority.

ARTHUR. Such as what?

MEDRAUT. Your signet, for example. Too serious a business altogether to be left to subordinates.

ARTHUR *takes off his ring, gives it to* MERLIN, *who hands it to* MEDRAUT.

MEDRAUT. *Iussa tua comprehendo et perficiam.*

Exit MEDRAUT. *A* COMPANION *comes in and takes away the dragon-standard.*

MERLIN (*singing*).

The father of the Prince of Gododdin was a Hercules in his great strength

His trunk was a rock of the sea-shore, a high beacon-tower was his head

Against the Picts beside my General his fist alone was an iron weapon.

Who won the Battle of the Caledonian Forest?

Arthur, and Gogyrvan his friend:

Gogyrvan the Huge they called him, he was a giant and now he is dead . . .

SCENE THREE

Ruins.

Enter GODODDIN *and* ANEURIN.

GODODDIN. He had his bowels and his bladder chopped out by a battle-axe – a matter of five or six years ago – he was fighting the Pictish pirates in the gorge of the Water of Leith. This is an unlooked-for pleasure, Chief Dragon. I was of course aware that your Army had lately moved into the neighbouring territory of Strathclyde. Your nephew the Prince of Strathclyde, do you know, regards himself as being at feud with me.

ARTHUR. I had not heard you were at feud. Why are you at feud?

GODODDIN. Oh, for no very good reason –

MERLIN (*singing*).

No very good reason ever when these Princes are at feud –

GODODDIN. – something in connection with my father and his father and a dispute about a concubine . . .

MERLIN (*singing*).

O Emperor of fallen Rome, tyrannical was your rule
But you ruled over one nation where now there are thirty-two.

GODODDIN. So you understand that Strathclyde is quite likely at any time to send a war-band into my land to ravage it. Likewise the heathen Picts out of Fife and East Lothian. My own war-band is courageous, but small. We are badly in need of protection.

ARTHUR. That is why I am here.

GODODDIN. For this season, however, we have already obtained the services of a strong army.

ARTHUR. *That* is why I am here.

He makes a sign to MERLIN *who hands the letter to* GODODDIN *who passes it to* ANEURIN.

You don't deny that you wrote it?

GODODDIN (*indicates* ANEURIN). He wrote it.

ARTHUR. When?

GODODDIN. When did you write it, Chief Poet?

ANEURIN. There is no precise date upon the document.

ARTHUR. Why?

GODODDIN. I am a Prince. But my land is poor. My own person is poor. This meagre diadem upon my head is the only regalia I possess. Not very many people here, and all that my father left me is my power over their lives. When I come in, when I go out, they bow down to me beside my doorpost. These English have set their foot at the farthest corner of my dominion. The men and women who live there are many miles from the rock of Dunedin. They do not see me, I do not see them, they do not bow down. They will not thank me if I come south with my war-band and bring battle as well as English into that farthest corner. The war-band will not thank me: it is not *their* homes they would be defending. Provided that the English and the Picts are kept out of Midlothian, my adulterated diadem will still remain here, upon my head.

ANEURIN. By Midlothian we mean all the land that we can see from the top roof-tree of this castle, he never walks out any further than that.

GODODDIN. I am afraid if I did they might pull off my diadem and some one would set up the cry that it is not made of real gold. Men who do not bow down would not scruple to keep their hands from my accoutrements. Before long I would have them all in here, carousing, within the threshold of my house.

ARTHUR. It is many years since I have caroused. Nevertheless at this moment I am inside of your door. I could turn around and whistle and have in my whole Army. Let alone the greedy warriors of my nephew Strathclyde.

ANEURIN. General, amongst these Princes in the northern part of Britain you have learnt how to ingratiate yourself with nobody – nobody! Oh, you hold us in contempt that we should wish to make friends with the English –

GODODDIN. We all hold one another in contempt, do we not? We all acknowledge it, so then ignore it. The word is this: within my door. So stay inside it, General, be my guest, be my friend – be my better friend than the English! Lord General, be my kinsman.

ARTHUR. Be your *what*!

GODODDIN. Let us calculate advantages, and also disadvantages, and let these learned men here note them down. Then we put them to the balance. You seek an opportunity to destroy your heathen enemy, with support and good friendship from all the land wherein you fight. I seek to keep my land, and in particular

Midlothian, inviolate from everyone. But if you attain your desire I cannot attain all mine. There will be a campaign throughout Gododdin and willy-nilly I shall be part of it. Then you and your Army will go, and you will leave my dominion enfeebled – for whom? Strathclyde.

ARTHUR. I do not think so.

GODODDIN. I do. He is a most orgulous Prince and he is not within your obedience.

MERLIN. True.

GODODDIN. But his younger brother is.

ARTHUR. You mean Medraut.

GODODDIN. Medraut. Medraut will have carried in front of him the dragon-banner of Rome one day, if, after your death, it is ever carried by anyone. My sister is a young widow, I would be glad to see her with a husband.

ARTHUR. God in Heaven!

ANEURIN (*aside*). God in heaven, but *I* would not!

Goods and gear the man gives me for the work that I perform. If the tears run out at my eyelids, what has that to do with him?

Aloud.

If Medraut and Gwenhwyvar
Within one blanket-bag were tied
It might well heal the feud
Between Gododdin and Strathclyde.

GODODDIN. Good.

ANEURIN.

If Medraut were the General
And Gwenhwyvar the General's wife
There would be here a fierce great Army
To protect Gododdin for all his life.

GODODDIN. Good again ... better ...

ANEURIN. That was only advantages. You did say to note down the disadvantages also.

According to your princely word
She may sleep with whomever you will.
But who is to say in the morning
Which one of them lies nearest the wall?

GODODDIN. Too obscure, and hypothetical. I was asking you for

common-sense – not for poetry. You are forgetting the terms of
your employment, young man. Well, General, what do you say to
it!

ARTHUR. Ignominious, unprincely, mercantile, you are the worst
kind of village money-lender – look at him, Merlin, can't you just
see him diverting the brook at night to flow over his patch of
ground and then to make the peasants pay him five bushels of
corn to draw one bucket of water –

MERLIN. Not good to be beside yourself, Lord General, keep
control –

ARTHUR. In time of drought he would do it, when the cattle and
sheep were stretched out panting by the roadside, flies in their
eyes and their black tongues protruding for drink –!

MERLIN. The General, you see, has never set eyes on your sister.
So how can we give an answer?

GODODDIN. She is here upon the rock of Dunedin. An arrange-
ment will be made to bring you together.

Exeunt GODODDIN *and* ANEURIN.

ARTHUR. I have heard something of this woman. Gwenhwyvar, do
you tell me, is her name?

MERLIN.
Gwenhwyvar the daughter of Gogyrvan the Huge:
Bad when little, worse when big.
I have heard they say that of her.

ARTHUR. I have heard that also. But I was told she said it of herself.
God knows what sort of horror he is concealing in his house. Did
she not murder her first husband?

MERLIN. It has been said.

ARTHUR. If young Medraut becomes allied in marriage to a territorial tribal Prince his undiluted loyalty to the integrity of my
Roman force can no longer be assumed . . . advantages . . . disadvantages . . . my nephew has loved many women but never for
very long. They come to him for the last time and they weep in his
tent all night and then off they go and that's all . . . I could marry
him to a three-eyed giantess, I don't believe he'd know the
difference, he wouldn't look that far up . . . and when all is said I
myself had one sister of whom I am heartily ashamed . . . Chief
Poet, find out this lady, put your eyes on her and your tongue at
her and then tell me what you think. (*He leaves.*)

SCENE FOUR

Seascape.

Enter ANEURIN, *strolling gloomily.*

MERLIN (*singing*).
    He does not wish to walk with me so I follow a little behind
    He walks by the roar of the northern water and not in a straight
       line.
ANEURIN (*suddenly calling*). Lady – oho – lady – it is myself, your
    poet here –!

> *There is an answering cry – as though from a good distance – two
> female voices.* ANEURIN *waves, and then stands expectantly.
> Running feet are heard.*

MERLIN (*singing*).
    Who are these who from the waves he can summon with one
       cry –
    Their robes clinging wet to their bodies and the salt water
       blinding their eyes?
ANEURIN (*his hand raised; in a loud clear voice, in the direction of the
running feet*).
    I declare three deeds of little wisdom upon the shore of the
      Firth of Forth:
    To entertain two violent robbers within one small enclosed
      court;
    To promise your sister in marriage to the General's Lieutenant,
      without offering her chance of one word;
    To go swimming in the steep cold tide when the night is about
      to fall.

> *The running feet have stopped running.* GWENHWYVAR *and*
> GWENDDYDD *enter, slowly. Their hair is wet and their clothes
> apparently only just thrown on.*

GWENDDYDD. The last one was not intended. She sat on a rock
    under the sunset and ordered me to comb her hair, the comb fell
    into the water.

MERLIN (*with a start; he stares fixedly at* GWENDDYDD). It is not possible . . . !

GWENHWYVAR. A golden comb. The only recollection of my husband that is worth anything at all. So I made her dive for it. She nearly drowned.

GWENDDYDD. We did not find it. But I was rescued.

GWENHWYVAR. We are frozen wet and very angry.

ANEURIN. At the loss of the comb or at the other thing that I told you?

GWENHWYVAR. Call it the loss of the comb. The General's Lieutenant is not after all the first to whom I have been promised.
Both old and young, they come and look at me
Without one word they turn and run from me.

GWENDDYDD. What else do you expect? You are a murderess.

GWENHWYVAR. You must not say that, girl. My first husband was murdered by the ungrateful sheep-herders of the region that he ruled. He protected their flocks against wolves and bandits, and when they were unable to pay him any longer for the services of his sword, they stretched a rope between two trees upon a road where he travelled after dark, and crash – the horse came down, the proud rider fell sideways.

GWENDDYDD. How was it the murderers were told which road he would travel and when?

GWENHWYVAR. I say nothing about that. His duty to his sheep-herders was no less than his love for his wife.
I cooked him a broth of good red pepper
To keep that love both hot and high
I laid the bowl in front of him
But in it he spied a fly.
He took up bowl and broth and spoon
And threw them in my eye.

GWENDDYDD (*suddenly sees* MERLIN).
That is a story we have all heard before.
I know a little man could tell you many such and more –
Merlin, come out – we have discovered you where you are!

MERLIN, *somewhat shame-faced, advances to the three of them. He bows to* GWENHWYVAR.

MERLIN. Madam, it is a high privilege to find myself presented to you. I offer you my humble service.

GWENHWYVAR. This lady is my companion and attendant. Her name is –

MERLIN. Gwenddydd. Well aware of it.

GWENHWYVAR (*suddenly giggling*). God help us – here's embarrassment.

GWENDDYDD. Aneurin Poet, my sweetheart, when you marry a wife and then go from her after so many years, how many I don't remember –

MERLIN. Fifteen.

GWENDDYDD. – and then you meet her again, half-naked, talking secrets with a friend, you yourself crouched in the corner like a spy – you will need to provide yourself with some class of deportment. So take note of him – he is your pattern.

ANEURIN. Master of his craft, accredited member of the College of Bards.

GWENHWYVAR. She tells me you used to hit her when she was great with child.

MERLIN. Yes, she would say so, wouldn't she?

GWENHWYVAR. So prove it.

GWENDDYDD. The result of course was a miscarriage.

MERLIN. Prove what?

GWENHWYVAR. So prove you never hit her.

MERLIN. Madam, I will be damned if I prove anything of the sort. I don't want to talk about this, it makes my skin burst out in blotches. Nobody told me she was living in Gododdin. Oh yes she has been travelling – 'at large' is a good word for it . . .

GWENHWYVAR. Why did you not murder him?

GWENDDYDD. He would have haunted me.

GWENHWYVAR. I have proved that superstition to be completely untrue.

GWENDDYDD. There was a time when he made music. I was in fear it might never go out of my head. Different consequence to murder a poet than to murder a –

GWENHWYVAR. Murderer. We'll talk no more of it. Merlin Chief Poet, will you tell me directly, what manner of man is the General's Lieutenant?

MERLIN. He is the leg upon which the General does not limp. He has been loved by many women, he has always refused to deliver himself into their hands.

GWENHWYVAR. Cold?

MERLIN. I am quite sure he could be kindled.

GWENHWYVAR. By me?

MERLIN. I hope not.

GWENHWYVAR. You appear not to want me to marry him. I thought it was all arranged.

MERLIN. By no means. My General is not yet decided.
　　All will depend
　　Upon what I recommend.
　　He will make up his mind
　　When I describe him what I find.

GWENHWYVAR. Describe me to myself as you will describe me to him.

MERLIN.
　　She is a short quick woman, white and black.
　　She has thick buttocks and a strong-built back.
　　Her teeth are strong and white but darkly stained.
　　Her hands are stained, invisibly, with blood.
　　She laughs at this and does not think it wrong.
　　I think she thinks she is the heroine of a song
　　Compelled to crime by cruelty. Not good
　　For politic expedience alone
　　To plunge a young man in a vat of brewing beer
　　And tell him that it's water. Mouth and ear and nose
　　He'll take it in in gallons, intoxicate his brain,
　　Drown in the dregs, or maybe scramble out
　　To lurch downstairs and wave his blade about
　　Till he has cut off six or seven good heads –
　　And then he'll say 'Who made these people dead?
　　I did not do it. I wanted to be clean.
　　I went to wash, now look at me, scum all over my skin!
　　Who put this sword into my hand?' he'll say,
　　'Someone has made a fool of me, someone will have to pay . . .'
　　I do not want him to look between *my* eyes upon that day.

SCENE FIVE

Ruins.

Enter ARTHUR *in a huge purple gown and plumed fur hat. His sword is slung round him, loose enough for him to lean on it like a walking stick. He is followed by* GODODDIN.

ARTHUR (*advancing on* GWENHWYVAR).
 If this lady is as dangerous
 As you report her to be
 If this lady is as dangerous
 As she reports herself to be –
 It is a feat for a champion
 To master her body and soul.
 It is a feat for a champion's poet
 To praise with his utmost skill.
 I am undisputed yet
 The champion of this land,
 I bear the sword of Maximus Emperor –
 It shall not pass out of my hand.
 The dragon-flag is yet mine
 The command of the horsemen is mine
 These tottering thighs will yet grip a saddle
 I am ignorant of the pain –
 These tottering loins will yet grip a strong woman
 Though it may astonish you to hear it said –
 Medraut shall *not* supplant me
 Though I love him as though he were my child.
 Here is a widow demanding to be wed
 But she warns against that wedding –
 Tongue and teeth in an evil smile –
 The attempt to be made on her
 Is to be made by the old man
 Not by the young. Except for a little while
 I had no child of my body that ever was alive.
 I had two wives and they died.
 I have had twelve children and they all died.

I inquired of priests and of wise men,
They could give me no reason
Except that I had been married
In a soft and peaceable season.
To compel those two young wives
To lie down and submit to me
Arthur son of Uther
Had no need for his rage and bravery.
Gododdin, you have given me refreshment –
The red wine has gone to my head.
I am both genial and jocular.
I call for your small scornful sister
To come now into my bed.

GODODDIN (*aside to* GWENHWYVAR.)
Here is a man at last
You are unable to terrify.
Lie down under him with composure –
Let us see if he will die.

GWENHWYVAR. If he does, will you be glad?

GODODDIN.
If he does or if he doesn't
My advantage will hold good.
Supposing that in your belly
The sperm of the dragon should breed –
There will be a giant of a new General
To supplant Medraut indeed.
When the father shall have died
Who else but I
Will be the guardian of the Army
And the preceptor of the child?
So much the worse, my dear,
For the aspirings of Strathclyde.

ARTHUR. It is agreed?

GODODDIN. You shall have the ceremony directly and a contract
can be drawn up, we have two poets in attendance, for what do we
wait?

ARTHUR. Priest.

GODODDIN. He is here.

He claps his hands. A MONK *enters.*

ARTHUR. Ring. I gave my signet to Medraut. I should not have done that.

ANEURIN (*taking a ring off his finger*). The Lord General may make use of this. Silver, not gold. Not much gold in Gododdin.

GWENHWYVAR (*aside to* ANEURIN). I gave you that ring.

ANEURIN (*aside to* GWENHWYVAR). So now it comes back again. It is a poet's duty to render up the riches of his heart without complaint.

> GWENDDYDD *has gone out and now returns with bridal orna-ments which she starts to put on* GWENHWYVAR. *A heavy white mantle with silver embroidery, a wide collar made up of a number of broad necklaces, a silver crown with glittering chains hanging down at each side.*

MERLIN (*singing*).
Until today my General
  maintained a policy that was ever firm
Conjuncture with these greedy Princes
  he ever claimed would do great harm.
Oh from where has come this thunder-burst, this unpredicted
  storm
That has twisted his head from his backbone and made a wind-mill out of his limbs?

> ANEURIN *has been writing rapidly on his tablets.* MERLIN *now goes over to him, reads what he has written, makes an amendment or two, and then hands the tablets to* ARTHUR, *with the pen.*

ARTHUR (*after a rapid perusal*). Agreed. (*He signs his name in big flourishing letters.*)

> MERLIN *then passes the tablets to* GODODDIN, *who makes no pretence at reading.*

GODODDIN. Agreed. (*He holds the pen awkwardly and makes his mark.*)

> ARTHUR *then seizes* GWENHWYVAR *by the wrist and leads her to the* MONK. *He puts the ring on her finger and they both kneel down.*

MONK. *In the Name of the Father and the Son and the Holy Spirit*:*

– my children, may God and the Evangelists watch over your blessed bed and render it fruitful to the continued advantage of the whole of this Christian land.

ARTHUR (*getting up*). Merlin: my purse.

> MERLIN *hands him a purse. The* MONK *holds out his hand and* ARTHUR *pours a great quantity of coins into it. Some of them fall on the floor and the* MONK *has to grub around quite a while to pick them all up.*

ARTHUR. There are men who call me heretic and hostile to the Cloth. Let them never dare say it upon this rock of Dunedin.

> *The* MONK *and* GODDODIN *go out.* MERLIN *and* ANEURIN *retire to one side.* GWENDDYDD *is still trying to put the finishing touches to* GWENHWYVAR's *costume.*

The ceremony is over, and you have not yet got her dressed! Leave her alone, girl, it is now time to be private.

> *Exit* GWENDDYDD.
>
> ARTHUR *unbuckles his sword-belt, throws off his cap, and divests himself of his gown. Underneath he is wearing his usual tunic and trews. He then advances upon* GWENHWYVAR *as though to start undressing her, but she prevents him with a strong gesture. Herself she pulls off her crown and collar and lets the mantle fall to the floor. (Already on the floor is the plaid which she had wrapped round her at her first entrance, and which* GWENDDYDD *has taken off to make way for the white mantle.) Underneath she has on a simple woollen gown. Her feet are bare.*

MERLIN (*singing*).
The bride and her bridegroom
Now enter their private room
To put on two faces that are not their own.

> *He picks up a mask and carries it to* ARTHUR. ANEURIN *picks up another one and carries it to* GWENHWYVAR.

> ARTHUR's *mask is a grinning demon – great tusk-teeth – bright red face – staring eyes – hair like a golliwog.*

> GWENHWYVAR's *is a kind of gorgon – protruding tongue – green hair of great length – staring eyes – livid white face. The* POETS *help their patrons to put on the masks and then stand back.*

ANEURIN (*singing*).
> They each desire the other should see
> What he or she would wish to be –

MERLIN (*singing*.
> This way there is no sort of victory.

ANEURIN (*singing*).
> Can the fish defeat the river –

MERLIN (*singing*).
> Or the river defeat the sea?

ARTHUR and GWENHWYVAR indulge in a very violent dance – a mime of battle rather than lovemaking – accompanied by as much thundering percussion as is available. They stamp themselves into exhaustion in a few moments and sprawl limply down on the floor. The dance should not be designed to work up to an obvious climax straight into full strength from the first steps and then suddenly finish. They do not end up lying too near each other.

MERLIN (*singing*).
> Alone and naked in the dark
> Grey goose and gander fold their greasy wings –
> Together they crouch down
> Upon the running stream –

ANEURIN (*singing*).
> The bride and bridegroom dream
> Of what they once have been.

BOTH POETS (*singing*).
> How strange is the change
> When no one is there to see . . .

The two POETS go out, passing àcross the middle of the stage. ARTHUR and GWENHWYVAR take off their masks and hand them to the POETS on their way out. ARTHUR kneels to pray.

GWENHWYVAR. What are you doing?

ARTHUR. What do you think I am doing?

GWENHWYVAR. Oh – he is saying his prayers – goodness. He did it last night and he is doing it again this morning . . . What do you say to Him then? Or rather, what does He say to you? Who dictates to whom the orders for the day?

ARTHUR. I never went into battle without asking for the help of

God. I never came out of the battle without informing Him of my gratitude.

GWENHWYVAR. Even when you did not conquer?

ARTHUR. There have been such occasions, yes – though I don't imagine you will have heard my Chief Poet singing songs about them. . . . Twelve great victories, girl, and now it is as though I am once again at the beginning of my life's work. Eternal victory belongs to God – it is not measured in terms of the lifetime of one man.

GWENHWYVAR. One man who knows full well he can never finally conquer. His life's work is worth nothing? So grey he has become, and scarred, and harsh all over his body. . . .

ARTHUR. I am not able to do anything better than what I have tried my best to do . . . I find myself to be a soldier, at this very particular time, when three-quarters of the world is starving crazy, roving all over for land on which to live, there is land here that was once fertile and can be so again, but it has to be defended or else it will be taken, first being made empty for those who crave to take it. I am a soldier, I make war, with good conscience, and that's it . . . No! You go too far, you are unjust, both to me and to yourself – you took delight, exceedingly, from my vigour in your bed – you were beyond measure wanton, you cried out, you demanded more.

GWENHWYVAR.

    Observe this disappointed man
    Believes himself to be the fresh cold rain
    And sunshine that will make the grass grow green.
    He stretches out his corded arms and cries:
    'Young woman, young woman strip off your clothes
    Upon my scaly breast lay down your head.
    I am the only champion of God.
    Permit yourself to be split in two –'
    The sword of Magnus Maximus goes through and through
    The blood flows down between the knocking knees
    And where it soaks into the ground so dry
    The golden corn shall spring up thick and high
    The fruits and flowers miraculously arise
    All creatures that God made
    Into this new-made garden come and feed . . .
    So too in the trap-hole of the night *you* cried

You also cried. I was awake. I heard –
The dragon's mouth fell open and there fell out certain words –
Do you remember what they were?

ARTHUR. This is not true, you are inventing – out of spite –

GWENHWYVAR. Why spite? Why not affection? Look, I will tell
you what you said: 'Lady' you said – but in the morning you call
me 'girl' – 'Lady, this bone is yours, to break or bend or mend!'

ARTHUR. I am perfectly certain I said nothing of the sort.

GWENHWYVAR.

Perhaps you were asleep.
Or else, without your clothes, without your sword.
Without your Army, and without your God,
Perhaps you had let yourself give yourself up
To what you used to be before
It came into your mind that making war
Was all the work that needed to be done.
To what great dragon-eating lady
Did you dedicate your bone?
It could not be to me –
Our marriage is expedient and political,
Also a kind of challenge to prove yourself still virile,
A feat for a champion to master me body and soul.
Your two dead wives? I have been told
Your love for them was very dry and cold.
The Virgin Mother of your Jesus Christ?
You know her worship must be always chaste –
In triumph of your furious lechery
You'd never think of *Her* most modest sovereignty.
So tell me who she was, as you would tell a friend.
If you tell me to whom you once did give
The beauty of your body when you were young,
I can tell you from now on you will live
Five times as free and twenty times as strong –

ARTHUR. My freedom and my strength are conferred upon me by
no one but –

GWENHWYVAR.

God. Oh, in the frosty morning, yes,
You kneel down and shiver,
You offer up your long petitions
With a grim disordered liver –

But I saw you at your prayers.
I said: 'Where is the power
I heard uttered in one short scream
Two inches from my ear?'
Oh, Gwenhwyvar was there
Dressed in nothing but her hair.
General, I tell you, if you believe that you believe
In the omnipotence of Christ, you are very much deceived.

She laughs wickedly. ARTHUR *takes two strong steps towards her and hits her on the side of the head – hard. She is knocked to the floor by the force of the blow. It takes her a while to get up. When she does so, she is shaking all over.*

GWENHWYVAR. Black-and-white your poet said I was. Black-and-white and red I am now. It is good to have a husband who knows how to improve my complexion.

ARTHUR. As you say, it is a frosty morning, you will need to wrap up well, a cloak of warm fur – keep you warm upon the horse. (*He picks up his purple gown and tosses it to her.*) We depart immediately for my Army. (*He takes his sword and his fur cap and goes out.*)

GWENDDYDD *comes in. During the ensuing dialogue she helps* GWENHWYVAR *to dress. She attempts to put the purple gown on her, but* GWENHWYVAR *rejects it and instead is wrapped up in her original plaid. The wedding ornaments and the white mantle are gathered up by* GWENDDYDD *and at some suitable juncture taken offstage, together with the purple gown.*

GWENHWYVAR.
My mother was an ill woman
She did my father great wrong;
He was merciful and kind to her
Although he was so strong.
His kindness and his mercy
Wounded her far worse
Than if he had ridden over her
And trampled her with his horse.

GWENDDYDD. Which is as much as to say that whatever they do to us, we are right and they are wrong.

Enter ANEURIN.

GWENHWYVAR (*laughing*). You had a father, he was a nobleman, you told me – did he say his prayers to Jesus?

GWENDDYDD. Every night, every morning. But my mother was not so certain.

GWENHWYVAR. Neither was mine, indeed.

GWENDDYDD. She told me stories that this land was once inhabited by huge ladies of great beauty.

GWENHWYVAR. Huge?

ANEURIN. When they walked through the forest, with the scrape of their rolling hips the tree-tops were broken off. The print of their feet created mountain tarns full of frogs and little fishes, the red eagles flew in and out of the tangles of their long hair, and when they shed tears it came down like storms of rain.

GWENDDYDD. But they were all driven out, you see, they were destroyed by armed men.

GWENHWYVAR. Starving crazy for land, I suppose. Once they took it they sat down upon it, they said, 'This has always belonged to us.' – and if the huge ladies they destroyed had left little daughters behind them, they took hold of those girls, and they said, 'Belongs to us, she has always belonged to us!' Is that the way it went? I'd call that story foolish. Who lay with the huge ladies that they should have daughters in the first place?

GWENDDYDD. As my mother explained it, once a year the seals would come out of the sea upon the beaches of the Hebrides, they would take off their sealskins, turn into men, and stay upon land for a night and a day. The women would take furiously from them all that they could get. Then back into the sea again, and once more they were seals, they swam about, they caught fish.

GWENHWYVAR. What happened if the huge ladies gave birth to a male child?

GWENDDYDD. He would be thrown into the sea, over the edge of the cliffs, and behold he was a seal.

GWENHWYVAR. Not at all. They pulled him to pieces and ate him. I have seen them in my dreams with the blood running out at the corners of their mouths, trickling down over their enormous white shoulders, hanging in drops from the points of their nipples. Oh, they ate him.

ANEURIN. They did not. He was compelled to bend his back and work – he dug the land, he brought forth food. And when the invaders came in, he bent his back again and he dug the land for *them*!

GWENDDYDD. Not true!

GWENHWYVAR. Great error!

GWENDDYDD. There was neither division nor degree upon the digging of the land –

GWENHWYVAR. No one for their own self held any title to the ground –

GWENDDYD. Indeed it is most doubtful whether any digging was done at all. Hunting and fishing and the gathering of fruit from trees and everyone did their share of it and everyone shared what was obtained.

ANEURIN. Are you certain of that?

GWENHWYVAR. Good God, poet, what's wrong with you, we are amusing ourselves with fairy-tales, we don't have to talk truth, you know!

ANEURIN. I don't know that it is truth, either what I said or what you said. But I am glad to discover that whatever happens *now* you both agreed at once that it should not have happened *then*. Which is, I suppose, the main purpose of a fairy-tale, even when we laugh at it . . . Lady, just at present I don't feel much like laughter. Lady, I am a man who will *not* dig and delve for the invader who has taken possession of *you*. I find you in the morning risen from his bed flushed as red as a ripe plum with the pleasure you have had from him. Your sovereignty over yourself has been betrayed, I can see that.

> And so, to prevent a base repetition
> I put on you this prohibition:
> You shall not laugh aloud in front of him
> Or open your wide mouth in front of any man
> Until you first have laid your hand on him
> With these words: 'I make the choice, it is my turn.
> I've chosen you: you are the one.'

You've never had the chance to do that for yourself, ever. Except in regard to me.

GWENHWYVAR. You don't count. You are my poet, it is my perquisite – but I tell you what you are not – you are not a Chief Bard. Therefore do not pretend to be, uttering out these sanctimonious prohibitions. How dare you! The only reason you ever had my love for three days was because you refused to have anything to do with that sort of nonsense –

ANEURIN. Lady, I did wrong and you are quite right.

GWENHWYVAR. I am? Then I forgive you. Come here, poet, you are forgiven. (*She kisses him.*)

ANEURIN. Not your poet. Not any more. I'm sorry, but I can't do it. From now on the learned Merlin must serve your turn for verse.

GWENHWYVAR. So what will you do? You will remain with Gododdin?

ANEURIN. To eat his bad bread and drink his vinegar after this would choke me to death. Improvise a verse to say good-bye to you, why don't I?

> There they both stand
> The quick green daughters of Branwen,
> Stand with their heads bowed
> And their hands folded humbly –
> Captive to the long sword
> As their mother was before them.
> For so short a time they could run and play.
> Now the garden is closed against them
> There remains only the spiked encampment.

Exits.

GWENHWYVAR. What do you think he meant by the 'Daughters of Branwen'? Aneurin Poet! What did you mean by – come back here and answer you inconsiderable bitter creature –!

GWENDDYDD. I know what he meant. The huge ladies my mother talked about, that was the name that they had. I had forgotten it.

GWENHWYVAR. No, there's more to it than that. My mother said to me – one day when she was cursing for what my father had not done to her, she said: 'Does a Daughter of Branwen have to live with this always?' I said: 'What's a Daughter of Branwen?' She said: 'Mind your business till you're old enough. When your father forbids you to play any more in the barnyard with boys, come to me and I'll explain.' But by the time that happened, you see, my mother was dead. So I never found out. . . .

GWENDDYDD. Did he hurt you when he hit you?

GWENHWYVAR. Yes. What the devil is the use of this poet full of

self-pity to put his prohibitions onto me? Does he not realize I
have put them myself, already?

Enter ARTHUR *in his war-coat,* MERLIN *and* GODODDIN.

GWENHWYVAR. Aha – the spiked encampment . . .

ARTHUR (*to* GODODDIN). So it is understood that your agreement
with the English leader is repudiated. But don't tell the English
leader. And your war-band, if I want it, is to be held ready for my
command.

GODODDIN. Understood.

MERLIN (*to* GWENDDYDD). Once we reach the military lines there
will be no reason for us to meet. You are in attendance upon my
lady, and that is all. Our tents are numerous and well spread-out.
Is that understood?

GWENDDYDD. It's understood.

Exeunt ARTHUR *and* MERLIN. GODODDIN *embraces* GWEN-
HWYVAR *and then* GWENDDYDD.

GWENHWYVAR (*singing*).
   O the cruel winter –
GWENDDYDD (*singing*).
   And the pain of its arrival –
ALL THREE OF THEM (*singing*).
   Young wives who will behave themselves
   Have small chance of survival . . .
   GODODDIN *goes out at one side, the women go out the other,*
   following ARTHUR.

SCENE SIX

Camp.

Enter MEDRAUT, BEDWYR *and* CARADOC. BEDWYR *is in his war-*
gear, MEDRAUT *in civilian clothes with his round cap stuck casually*
on the back of his head.

BEDWYR. His name is Caradoc.

MEDRAUT. Name of a great chieftain.

BEDWYR. He is not a great chieftain. He keeps a small-holding with twelve cows in the valley of the River Tyne.

MEDRAUT. Yes.

BEDWYR. He says the young soldiers you have recruited for your new regiment have ransacked his house and yard, and slaughtered three of his beasts and cooked them.

MEDRAUT. Yes . . . Caradoc, I know the house. I also know that a whole troop of the heavy cavalry was quartered there until last week. How many cows did *they* slaughter?

CARADOC. Lord –

MEDRAUT. How many?

CARADOC. Lord, they slaughtered nine.

MEDRAUT. So now you have none left.

CARADOC. None but the little calf, lord, and not a drop of milk for her now. She cannot stand upon her legs.

MEDRAUT. Why in God's name do you make such a hollering about the loss of three cows when you said not one word about nine?

CARADOC. Lord, the heavy cavalry are the General's own men. We know what it is they do.

MEDRAUT. And the young soldiers –?

CARADOC. For them it is quite different. They wore a brass earring in the left ear.

MEDRAUT. What?

BEDWYR. You have recruited your men from a certain clan across the river that is regarded by *his* clan as unclean. Therefore three cows eaten by them is more than three times as bad as the nine cows that we took.

MEDRAUT. We?

BEDWYR *snorts and looks sideways.*

Caradoc, man, there is nothing at all I can do about this. If I caught the thieves, I could punish them, tie them up and whip them, but your three cows would be inside of them, I would be punishing them too. Think of it this way: indeed the soldiers take your cattle but the English would take your life. While the soldiers are here the English can't get at you. Which would you rather?

CARADOC. Lord, my cattle *are* my life. And if I am to be beholden to anyone for my safety I had a great deal better not take it from a brass earring in the left ear.

MEDRAUT. But what possible reason can you have for –?

CARADOC. I don't know. I don't talk to them. The rich man who is lord of my land has told me they eat children.

MEDRAUT. Cows.

CARADOC. Children! He is lord of their land too. He ought to know what he talks about, oughtn't he?

MEDRAUT (*taking a gold bracelet from his wrist*). Look, here is a piece of gold. You exchange this in a good market, you could get yourself fifteen cows.

CARADOC. What use is it to me? This winter there is no market here, good or bad. Nothing but your war. May God destroy the whole herd of you.

Exit CARADOC, *with the bracelet. Enter* DYLAN, *with his weapons. He wears an earring in his left ear.*

DYLAN. Lord, he was abusive. Will I go after and cut his throat?

MEDRAUT. You will not. Dylan, do you eat children?

DYLAN. I do not, lord.

MEDRAUT. He says you do.

DYLAN. I happen to know, lord, that he and his people prostitute themselves with their own cattle in the pasture.

MEDRAUT. They do *what*! Who told you that?

DYLAN. It is well known. The man who collects his rent from my father has seen them at it, often.

MEDRAUT. Dylan, you are a great fool to believe such a thing. Yet for all that, I am more satisfied with the men of the one earring than with any others I have enlisted. (*To* BEDWYR.) Of course I know that you are not. They do disturb your regularity.

Enter ARTHUR *and* COMPANIONS, *in their war-gear.*

ARTHUR. And moreover they disturb mine . . . There are too many women in the camp. Who gave the Companions permission to have their wives and families with them?

MEDRAUT. You did, uncle. You said it was unlikely there would be a battle before the winter was over, so the men might as well keep themselves as warm in bed as you were. You said it the moment you arrived back from Dunedin with the lady Gwen-hwyvar.

ARTHUR. Changed my mind about it, haven't I . . . ? A ship has come in this morning to the Englishmen's landing-place.

FIRST COMPANION. We have just had a smoke-signal from the hilltop to say so. Full of armed men and barrels of stores.

SECOND COMPANION. The third such vessel in ten days.

ARTHUR. It is evident they are not deterred by the weather from reinforcing themselves ... (*He notices* DYLAN.) Good God, boy, who is this?

MEDRAUT. His name is Dylan Red-Nostril, he is Chief Captain of my skirmishers.

ARTHUR. And you are my Lieutenant. And he is your Chief Captain ...

MEDRAUT. Yes ... Unfortunately the weather is not so wild as we had hoped for this time of the year.

BEDWYR. God has laid low the great waves for the purpose of punishing Britain.

ARTHUR. Oh, He has? He has informed you privately that that is what He has done?

BEDWYR. Not so much a positive statement, General, but merely a remark that it could be said to be so. Or else, why, after all that this Army has achieved, should the heathen put forward so huge an invasion once more?

SECOND COMPANION. Are they not afraid of us?

FIRST COMPANION. They must be. They must know what happened to the Saxons in the south.

ARTHUR. Oh they know it; but afraid of it? Listen: Out of the back of Germany, over thousands of miles of the Scythian wilderness, every nation, every tribe is on the move towards the west. Nothing to eat, you see. And so those next to the western water get pushed into the water. And being people of good contrivance, they provide themselves with ships. By the time they get to Britain they are men who have no hope left – who are they under such a fate to be afraid of men like us?

MEDRAUT. Uncle, you talk philosophy.

ARTHUR. Sense.

MEDRAUT. Did you get it out of a book?

ARTHUR. I did not. I got it from a party of Baltic merchants in Dunedin – I drank with one or two of them as a preparation for my wedding night ... out of one wine jug I befitted myself for two battles at one time! Very good: I fought the first one. So now for the second! We don't sit idle any longer. We take some action.

MEDRAUT. Such as what?

ARTHUR. We must draw him out of his entrenchment, don't you see? Get that hostage – get him quick!

One of the COMPANIONS *goes out.*

ARTHUR. This new regiment of yours – how complete is it – how reliable?

MEDRAUT. You have seen us at our exercise.

ARTHUR. Midsummer Fair in an upland village. Pony races bare-back for the prize of a cockerel, yelping and screaming and all the dogs running after, rag-tag and bob-tail . . .

MEDRAUT. Uncle, that's exactly how I want them to be, but I haven't got enough of them yet.

The COMPANION *returns with the* ENGLISHMAN. *The latter's blindfold is removed.*

ARTHUR (*taking no notice of the new arrival*). Then go and get some more.

MEDRAUT. I have scoured the whole country between here and the Cleveland Hills –

ARTHUR. Then take yourself elsewhere, take your whole regiment off, make up its numbers in some appropriate mountain region, and above all, improve its discipline. I suppose it is because you wish to set them an example that you are wearing your cap on the back of your head?

MEDRAUT. My cap – what . . . ?

ARTHUR. Put it straight, boy, when you talk to me . . . Now, I want you to tell this malodorous ruffian that I am going to send him back to his chief.

MEDRAUT. *Ure wisa wile eow agiefan eowran heretogan.*

ARTHUR. I have considered the matter of the agreement with Gododdin, they are within their rights to be here, it would not be honourable for me to make war on them. Tell him that.

MEDRAUT. *Ure wisa sægth thæt ge sindon hider mid rihte cumen. Treowleasnes wære gif he eow feahte.*

The ENGLISHMAN, *astonished, bows stiffly.* ARTHUR *laughs, shakes his hand, and claps him on the back.*

ARTHUR. To be frank with you, Medraut, I don't want your regiment about this camp any longer. Carlisle is the place for them.

Get the Prince of Strathclyde to give you permission to recruit
among his hills.

MEDRAUT. He won't let me.

ARTHUR. He won't let *me*, that's for certain: but God help us, you
are his brother ... Bedwyr, how many men would we risk to lose
if we made a frontal attack on the biggest stockade?

BEDWYR. Without a breaching-engine? We'd lose the lot.

ARTHUR. A breaching-engine we can make.

FIRST COMPANION. Not one man in the camp has ever seen such a
thing. Would you have us go to Constantinople to find out what
they look like?

ARTHUR. Now look you, man, we improvise – improvise – don't
forget that I have read the book of Titus Livius! I want a good
strong engine built. I mean to see it in working order by the Feast
of the Nativity ... Nephew, you will take with you to Carlisle
every woman, every child, every sutler, every wagon full of useless gear that is cluttering up this camp. We are planning for a big
battle, we don't want anyone around who is going to hamper my
tactics. Bedwyr, you take two troops of horse and establish a
stockaded camp upon the coast ten miles to the north of the
heathen stronghold.

BEDWYR. Whatever for?

ARTHUR. It is my tactic, sir! I shall have need of a small reserve ...
I thought I said this barbarian was to be sent back to his leader.
Get him out of it.

FIRST COMPANION. Blindfold him, Chief Dragon?

ARTHUR. No. With all due courtesy. We have told him we are his
friends.

FIRST COMPANION (*to* ENGLISHMAN). Come along then, you get
out of it. Go!

ENGLISHMAN. *Nane Bryttwealas næron treowfæste, ac ge beoth ealle
ofslægene.*

ARTHUR. And what was that he said?

MEDRAUT. Said we would all be killed. He called us Welshmen.

ARTHUR. M'm.

MEDRAUT. It is a word they have for us. It means 'foreigner' and it
also means 'slave'.

ARTHUR. So you discern, from that one word of theirs, the entire
life of such beasts of prey.

MEDRAUT. Moreover, he said that we were all without honour ...

Now, uncle, perhaps you will be so good as to stop contradicting
yourself and to explain what you think you are doing?

ARTHUR. Aha, I am old but I have mastered a hot young woman.
Not one word out of her since she first rolled and squealed
beneath me, at Dunedin, between the blankets . . . And I've confused *you* with my cunning tactics: so what do you think I have
done for *him*? Do we make war, do we retreat, do we split up the
Army, do we – what do we do? He goes through the lines with his
eyes uncovered, what is he going to see? The rag-tag and bob-tail
at their exercise upon the moor! He will tell them all about it over
there, they will disbelieve it, they will argue, they will finally get
drunk – and then they will come out. Their brains are churned-
up mud, you know, very slow they are indeed, but in the end
they *move*. We must be ready for that move. My calculation is the
week before the Feast of the Nativity. At the beginning of that
week I want your regiment, complete in numbers, to be wander-
ing at large between here and Carlisle – keep closely in touch
with me and prepare to bring them *anywhere* – at great speed – as
soon as I give the order.

MEDRAUT. But Bedwyr and his camp –?

ARTHUR. Oh yes, he sets it up. But we don't put two troops in – we
put *squadrons*. And not to the north of them either. Upon the
coast towards the south.

BEDWYR. The breaching-engine?

ARTHUR. Oh forget that!

MEDRAUT. And the women and children?

ARTHUR. That order holds good. To Carlisle.

MEDRAUT. *All* the women?

ARTHUR. All . . . Put your cap on straight – you are my officer.
(Exit)

BEDWYR.

Companions, we do not need
To look at each other with such surprise.
The new tactic of Chief Dragon has now been devised.
We obey his orders, he will succeed.

Exeunt BEDWYR *and* COMPANIONS.

DYLAN. Lord, the General does not want us about his camp any
longer.

MEDRAUT. Oh, that's only what he said.

DYLAN. Yes, lord, but he did say it.

Exeunt MEDRAUT *and* DYLAN.
Enter MERLIN *on the forestage, hurrying across.*

MERLIN (*calling*). Chief Dragon – call Medraut back! Not to let him go to Carlisle, Chief Dragon –!

Enter ARTHUR, *meeting* MERLIN.

ARTHUR. Not? And why not?

MERLIN. Not appropriate. I am your poet, I talk truth. Other than that, I can give you no good reason . . .

ARTHUR. Nor have you given me a single good poem for a matter of ten years. Fifteen years. Twenty. (*Exits.*)

MERLIN.

> I know that what he said is as true as what I say.
> I do not intend to refuse to take my pay.
> Hurt and blind and three parts ignorant
> I nonetheless must set my mind to hold this blind and ignorant General
> Erect and tall against the ebbtide and the flood – if he should fall
> Five hundred years of history will all be overwhelmed,
> Swilled away to nowhere in a pagan bog of blood and mud . . .
> The time has long gone past I should think of composing a poem.
> Yet goods and gear the man gives me for the work that I perform;
> If the tears run out at my eyelids, what has that to do with him?

Exit.

SCENE SEVEN

Fort.

Enter ANEURIN. *His clothes have deteriorated. He carries a worn-out traveller's bag. During the scene a number of women, soldiers' wives, pass in and out with bundles of personal luggage, crying children, etc.*

Some of them sit down and occupy themselves with various domestic tasks.

ANEURIN (*singing*).
>   I did not know which way to go when I went out of Gododdin's
>   house.
>   At random I went west, sore-footed I went to the south.
>   Men as poor as me did feed me – when they could not I did
>   without.
>   The fort at Carlisle was half in ruins but it sheltered one man
>   with a roaring mouth –
>   Strathclyde had come down to inspect his property:
>   oh how he did strut and shout!

STRATHCLYDE'S VOICE (*shouting offstage*). Where is he, where is
he? Comes into my fort, does he, brings with him a whole regiment – but take note that he does not come to *me* . . . !

ANEURIN (*singing*).
>   I did not tell him I was a poet –
>   he already had one, so I found.

Enter STRATHCLYDE *and* TALIESIN.

STRATHCLYDE. So young Medraut is come back to us – the bold,
golden soldier – I am astonished he can pluck up the nerve!

He notices ANEURIN.

And who are *you* – you are Arthur's man – you are Medraut's –
what are you?

ANEURIN. No, master, I am a traveller, I took refuge here from the
rain. The watchman at the gate did not prevent me.

STRATHCLYDE. Then he should have done. The very birds of the
air think they can make use of this fort as a damned resthouse
upon their frantic passagings!

Enter MEDRAUT *and* DYLAN.

So here you are and what do you pay me for the convenience you
are obtaining here?

MEDRAUT. Dear brother, we are obtaining convenience, are we?
God, but that's good news – I was afraid you would not approve
of my recruiting in your land.

STRATHCLYDE. I am talking about the continued use of this fort by

your overweening Roman General! And as for the recruiting –
no! Absolutely no! I will not allow my people to be hauled into a
war by Arthur in defence of my inherited blood-enemy. No!

MEDRAUT. Not by Arthur. Me. My regiment.

STRATHCLYDE. 'Regiment'! You see, he makes no bones, within
the first two minutes he meets me, to throw out his Roman words!

MEDRAUT. Better not to call it a regiment. Why don't we call it a
'Host'? I want to muster to my colours the young men of Strathclyde under the chieftains of Strathclyde, we will supersede the
Roman cavalry just as you and your fellow-Princes have super-
seded the Roman Governors and the Emperor who gave them
their pay.

TALIESIN. 'Supersede' is no good. The ancestors of Strathclyde
were rulers of their tribe before the Romans were ever heard of.

MEDRAUT. So we will not say 'supersede'. 'Resurrection' is a better
word.

STRATHCLYDE. The native spirit of this Island has never been
dead, never.

MEDRAUT. Then – 'Brought out of an alien slumber to feel once
more our ancient blood and power'?

STRATHCLYDE. That's better. That's very good!

MEDRAUT. I thought it might catch you.

STRATHCLYDE. And it will be *your* Army –

MEDRAUT. Host.

STRATHCLYDE. My brother's Host – oh, very good! It will *not* be
the regiment of the Lieutenant of the great General.

Enter GWENHWYVAR *and* GWENDDYDD.

Yet nevertheless you intend to assist Gododdin . . .

He confronts GWENHWYVAR.

Your brother is my blood-enemy, lady – yet you swing yourself in
to the hall of my fort as though you owned it!

GWENHWYVAR. Are you telling me you are demanding me to go –
turning out your uncle's wife? You complain about my entitle-
ment to warm my feet upon your hearthstone!

GWENDDYDD. He says you have inherited your father's feud against
him.

GWENHWYVAR. Inherited more than that! I've inherited my
mother's kinship. And by virtue of that kinship I demand my
right to stay here.

STRATHCLYDE. Mother? Kinship? First I'd heard of it. What in God's name does she think she is bawling about? Medraut?

MEDRAUT. I don't know.

GWENHWYVAR. Oh, do you not then –? But you should!

GWENDDYDD. But they should!

GWENHWYVAR. I had a mother – quite remarkably – who was married to your blood-enemy –

GWENDDYDD. And she in her turn had a mother as well –

GWENHWYVAR. And that one had a sister –

GWENDDYDD. And that sister went in wedlock to a man called the Prince of Cornwall, Lord Gorlois was his name –

GWENHWYVAR. And Prince Gorlois and his wife had three daughters, very beautiful, and one of them married –

MEDRAUT. And one of them married the Prince of Strathclyde, who was our father, and we are two of his sons. We know that much.

STRATHCLYDE. Of course we know that much – but all the rest of it – what – mother and a mother and a sister and three daughters – Taliesin?

TALIESIN. My lord?

STRATHCLYDE. Upon matters of genealogy you are supposed to be expert. Is what she says correct?

TALIESIN. Quite correct, my lord.

STRATHCLYDE. Oh . . . I have never heard of a pedigree before that consisted of nothing but women.

TALIESIN. It is customary among the Picts –

STRATHCLYDE. Filthy pagan copulators! Madam, you have a strange sense of humour in this Christian fort! However, you are my uncle's wife, you are my kinswoman. You are welcome to stay in Carlisle for as long as you wish.

GWENHWYVAR. We have no choice.

GWENDDYDD. We have been sent here.

MEDRAUT. By their husbands. All along with the redundant baggage-wagons from the camp.

STRATHCLYDE. Who is this one? Who's *her* husband?

GWENDDYDD.

I haven't got one. But if you prowl and scout
Among the numerous tents all well spread out.
A certain careful spider you may chance to meet –
He spins a strange web that could trip up your feet.

What does he catch in it? Dead alliteration, evaporated rhymes
That have hung in the cold air for a very long time.
A poet or two once uttered them, didn't like them, and left
them behind . . .
TALIESIN. Oh yes, of course – she's Merlin's wife – (*Aside to*
STRATHCLYDE.) – well, well, I would not have known her . . .

He sees that GWENHWYVAR, *who has just noticed* ANEURIN,
has gone over to embrace him – GWENDDYDD *does the same.*

My lord – will you take a look at *that*!

But STRATHCLYDE *has moved away and is having a confidential
word with* MEDRAUT.

STRATHCLYDE. Gododdin's sister can't be pregnant yet? Or can
she? Do you think that he is capable?
MEDRAUT. No business of mine, is it, whether he is or whether he
isn't?
STRATHCLYDE. Very much your bloody business, boy – suppose
she breeds a son?
MEDRAUT. Suppose she does?
STRATHCLYDE. It was always my opinion, saving myself from the
sin of blasphemy, that the Evangelist was not kind to the memory
of King Herod. You want to put that proposition to the rambling
boys of Strathclyde, when you recruit them on my mountains.
MEDRAUT. I thought you would not permit me?
STRATHCLYDE. You thought wrong, boy. I now know better.

TALIESIN *comes up to* STRATHCLYDE *in great excitement.*

TALIESIN. My lord, I give you warning: I have recognized that
vagabond. He is –
STRATHCLYDE. He is a poor wayfarer who has petitioned the hos-
pitality of Strathclyde. Unless he commits here some observable
crime, he is to be treated beneath my rooftree with full respect
and princely dignity. Medraut, we will confer with the captains of
my war-band and find out in which valley you will discover the
best men for your Host.

Exeunt STRATHCLYDE, TALIESIN, MEDRAUT, *and* DYLAN.

SCENE EIGHT

Mill.

ANEURIN (*singing*).

> I have made my own discovery in the Principality of Strath-
> clyde:
> A broken mill-house by the river not far from the fort of
> Carlisle
> – And in that broken house – for a wonder she is still alive –

Mill

It is years and years since we all heard she had gone off to the
woods and died –

In that house is a broken old woman. They say she has the evil
eye.

MORGAN *hobbles in, supporting herself on a stick.*

MORGAN. Why would I not have it? The Prince of Strathclyde is
my nephew, my own dear sister's son, and he will not even grant
me a little dingy corner in his fort where I could sit and dip my
bread into the soup and curse him for his sovereignty! When I
was young this land was ruled by other men: there was nothing
they would not do for Morgan . . . Gododdin's poet? You learnt
your poetry from whom? Merlin? Taliesin?

ANEURIN. Not any of those.

MORGAN. No – they have no truth in them . . . and old Arthur the
General, my own dear mother's hedgehog child – does he live or is
he dead? Has the big battle not yet happened that is to break
his banner in two?

ANEURIN. Not yet.

MORGAN. Not yet . . . they wouldn't tell me, even if it had. (*She
sees* GWENHWYVAR.) Oh, I know who *she* is – with her eyes like
green gooseberries – 'Bad when little, worse when big' – five and
twenty years ago behind the bushes near her father's fort she
would lift up her skirt for all the naughty little boys.

> And did they see
> What they were looking for?
> Why else did they fall to broken bones
> Sticks and stones and bloody weeping war?

Still at it, are you? If not, then why not? Old Morgan will tell you
the way . . .

GWENHWYVAR. And Gwenhwyvar will tell old Morgan she should
get about and mind her business –

MORGAN (*cackling*). Until she's old enough –? God protect us, poor
old Morgan is quite old enough for anything.

The question is – are you? So sit down quiet, dear daughter of
Gogyrvan's wife, till I have talked with my young poet.

GWENHWYVAR. *My* poet.

MORGAN. Mine. *All* of them are mine.

ANEURIN. They *were* yours, a long time ago. Not any more, old
lady. I am the only one left, I think.

MORGAN. And all the rest belong to Christ and to the men of the long sword. The black ravens are aware of it and they sharpen their beaks. What words have you put together that will prove to me you are my man . . . ?

ANEURIN. Words – I – er –

MORGAN. He is amazed, he begins to stutter. So I will give back to you your own words. Correct the old woman if her memory slips a little (*She sings*.)

> My house
> Is a bad house
> Black dark
> And the fire is cold
> Who is the man
> Who sits astride my roof
> Grips it with his knees
> He is far too strong
> Far too crooked
> Far too old
> Been there far too long
> I cannot get him down –

ANEURIN. That's right – I *did* make that song –

MORGAN (*singing*).

> Try, try –

ANEURIN (*singing*).

> He spits in my eye

MORGAN (*singing*).

> Pull at him, drag.
> Get hold of his leg –

ANEURIN (*singing*).

> Squats crooked up there forever
> For all that I can do
> Why don't you help me?

MORGAN (*singing*).

> No no, it is up to you!

ANEURIN. How is it that you know it and that you know that I made it?

MORGAN. Oh, but it is very well known and so is the other one – 'John Baptist and his cloth of hair' – I live here in secret but my ears are as long as those on a black rabbit. The question is this, you see, my dear, songs that are sung only in secret are not heard by everyone, even though everyone sings them.

ANEURIN. But why only in secret?

MORGAN. Look at him – he has forgotten how his own poetry concludes! Go on, boy, sing to the end of it.

ANEURIN (*singing*).

Very well then I have no choice
And nowhere else to turn
But to turn to the glow of the cold fire
Blow it up till it begins to burn
Up and up till the chimney is red-hot
Upon the thatch the sparks will fly
Upon the wall the flames will catch –

ANEURIN *and* MORGAN (*singing together*).

All that I ever desired will be thoroughly on fire
And in that fire this bad old man will die!

ANEURIN. Do you know that all that I meant by that song was an abuse of the fool Chief Poet to whom I was apprenticed as a pupil?

MORGAN. Doesn't matter what you meant by it. What matters is what it says. In little dripping cottages and forest shelters from the Firth of Clyde to Bodmin Tor there are men and women who sing that song and it says to them one thing. The dragon-banner must be broken and the Daughters of Branwen called home.

GWENHWYVAR. And who are the Daughters of Branwen?

MORGAN. *You* ask me that? Did your mother never tell you? Your poet will have been told – I don't know where he will have got it from, but he will have learnt it from somebody as disreputable as he is. Put the question to him.

ANEURIN. Yes, I can answer it. I was taught it by a blind beggar on the top of the Pentland Hills. I don't believe a word of it. In my opinion he was mad.

MORGAN. Made mad by what he knew. Just like old Morgan. Tell her.

ANEURIN. Two thousand years before I was born, Branwen was the sister of the Blessed Hero Bran. She was more than his sister, she was also his wife. They did such things in those days – oh, shame-less – but they were Kings and Queens – it was permitted. There are women all over Britain who can trace themselves back, childbed by childbed, to the childbed of Branwen herself where she brought forth her brother's daughter. And these women tell their own daughters – but they do not tell their sons. At any given time there is alive, in this Island, one woman somewhere who is the heiress to the throne and crown of Branwen – perhaps she is aware of it, perhaps not. But it is believed by many ignorant people –

MORGAN. *Not* in the palaces of Princes believed, but in all the secret places, where the people are thin and small. Not necessarily ignorant – my love, don't forget: it is your songs that they have by heart.

ANEURIN. It is believed that when her time has come, this lady will declare herself: she will choose for herself a man, and he will be the Secret King of the Island of the Mighty, he will be Bran, re-incarnate! Like Bran, he will come to his death: like Bran, he will do great deeds.

MORGAN. How did Bran come to his death – do you remember?

GWENHWYVAR. There are very many legends –

MORGAN. I will tell you the one that is true. Men of the long sword came in their black boats across the water. And their chieftain violated Branwen. Bran fought against him, he had only his bare hands, he was defeated, he was killed.

ANEURIN. So they buried his head.

MORGAN. *Branwen* buried his head, and from then on – she and her daughters – they have lived in perpetual slavery. The one who is to be Queen is chosen at her birth, by those who are instructed. There are certain signs – not easy to be recognized. When the child is a little older there are certain things she must remember. If she does not remember, then the whole business must be forgotten – and that would be the end of me. Tell me what *you* remember.

GWENHWYVAR. Me?

MORGAN. When you were a little girl and very dirty, were you never with grown-up ladies – perhaps in a private garden or the glade of a green wood – did you never play this game –? It is *not* to be forgotten . . .

Daughter dear daughter oh what are you looking for?

GWENHWYVAR.

An apple-tree in an orchard oh that is what I am looking for.

MORGAN. She has it! She has it exact!

What will you do when you find it, dear daughter?

GWENHYVAR.

I will call out the white stag that runs wild beneath the branches.

MORGAN.

What will you do to the stag when you catch him?

GWENHWYVAR. Catch him –? I don't know . . . oh yes: the golden collar!

MORGAN.

Which hand?

GWENHWYVAR.

The right hand.

MORGAN.

And what about the left hand?

GWENHWYVAR.

I will feed the fierce wolf who will jump upon my stag –

Ow – ow – ow – ow – ow – ow and they're all dead!

That bit used to frighten me.

MORGAN. Yes, it was meant to. There are more things I can tell you, more games yet to be played . . .

The old man climbs the quaking hill

One leg well and one leg ill –

But not in front of *him*.

Exit MORGAN.

GWENHWYVAR. Oh, what did all that mean?

ANEURIN. What do you think that it meant?

GWENHWYVAR. You don't think it meant –

ANEURIN. Most certainly it did.

GWENHYWVAR. *I* am the Daughter of Branwen? I am the Queen of the whole of Britain?

GWENDDYDD. And where *is* the whole of Britain? They should all be on their knees in front of you. I don't see a single one – except him, and he's your perquisite.

GWENHWYVAR. Very true. But at all events it's a piece of know-ledge that is both pleasant and warm. Keep it tight wrapped around yourself, what do you need with a husband? What else can I do with it?

ANEURIN. You could give it to someone.

GWENHWYVAR. Who?

ANEURIN. Not for me to say. But whoever he is, he will be King. I therefore recommend you to choose him very, very carefully.

GWENHWYVAR. But of course I would do that. Have I not always been fastidious?

ANEURIN. No. (*He goes out.*)

GWENDDYDD. Jealous he is already. First it was Arthur that vexed him and now it is an old old fairy-tale –

GWENHWYVAR. Not a fairy-tale – no, girl, it's good history: Bran the Blessed – oh, he lived, and he was Defender of this land.

GWENDDYDD. Arthur son of Uther lays claim to the title.

GWENHWYVAR. Can you imagine what the son of Uther was like when he was young? He might well have been worth the choosing in those days, don't you think so?

SCENE NINE

Fort.

Enter MEDRAUT *and* DYLAN. GWENHWYVAR *looks at* MEDRAUT

GWENHWYVAR. Do you know – he has not spoken to me since we rode out of his uncle's camp?

GWENDDYDD. Have you spoken to him?

GWENHWYVAR. I had other things to think about. And at all events, why should I? What is he but a man of the long sword – no better than the old dragon himself. Tell him so.

GWENDDYDD. Who – me –?

GWENHWYVAR. Yes, you, girl, go on, tell him.

MEDRAUT (*deep in conversation with* DYLAN). I can't understand it – they can't all have run off into the hills –

DYLAN. Village after village, and not one young man left in them fit to be recruited. I was told that Strathclyde has lately led his fighters to a great disaster against the Picts, and they will have no more of such leadership.

MEDRAUT. But that is exactly why I call upon them to come and to join with *me* –

GWENHWYVAR. I said you are to go and tell him. So do it.

MEDRAUT (*seeing the women*). What's the matter?

GWENDDYDD (*giggling*). She says you are a sort of murderer and no better than the old dragon.

MEDRAUT. I see . . . So you tell her that she too is a notorious murderess, which is why the old dragon married her and would not let me do it. Now will you leave me alone, please – I want to talk to my officer . . . (*To* DYLAN.) Go back again to that valley, don't bother with the young men, talk to the old ones, I don't think they have the least idea of what it is I'm trying to do –

GWENHWYVAR. What is it you are trying to do?

MEDRAUT. Madam: with some difficulty, I am trying to conduct my military affairs. I would be very much obliged if –

GWENHWYVAR. Oh, the devil with that. Captain, the Lieutenant-General has given you your instruction. Go back again up to that valley. Go back again at once.

> *Exasperated,* MEDRAUT *tips the wink to* DYLAN, *who grins, and goes out.*

I asked you a direct question. For what reason do you evade it?

MEDRAUT. I didn't know I had evaded it.

GWENHWYVAR. I said: what are you trying to do?

MEDRAUT. I am trying to recruit soldiers. You know that perfectly well.

GWENHWYVAR. Yes, but for whose Army?

MEDRAUT. There is only the one Army. True, each Prince has his own useless war-band, but there is only one *Army* – it is the Red Dragon Army of Britain – and –

GWENHWYVAR. And my husband is the General.

MEDRAUT. He won't be for much longer.

GWENHWYVAR. What –?

MEDRAUT. What –? For God's sake, woman, consider his age! When he dies, what will happen must be thought upon by his Lieutenant.

GWENHWYVAR. And what has the Lieutenant thought?

MEDRAUT. A great many things.

GWENHWYVAR. Tell me one of them . . . Don't evade it.

MEDRAUT. Very well then . . . After the Battle of Badon, it was the best of all his battles, your husband could so easily have made himself into an Emperor. Had he done so, three-quarters of his present trouble would not be upon his head.

GWENHWYVAR. Why didn't he?

MEDRAUT. I don't know. It was offered. He has given me no satisfactory explanation for his refusal.

GWENHWYVAR. The great ancestor Magnus Maximus did not refuse, did he?

MEDRAUT. And then he went and lost everything by attempting to march upon Rome. Had Maximus but contained himself he could have ruled over Britain for the rest of his life. He had the absolute loyalty of every man in the Island.

GWENHWYVAR. How did he get it?

MEDRAUT. His benevolence, his wisdom, his courage, I wouldn't wonder.

GWENHWYVAR. The devil with that. I was the woman who married him and that was all that it was.

MEDRAUT. I have heard that his wife was a British Princess.

GWENHWYVAR. His wife was the Daughter of Branwen, that's who.

MEDRAUT. She was what? I don't follow you.

GWENDDYDD. Who told you she was the Daughter of Branwen?

GWENHWYVAR. No one told me.

    It just came into my head
    Like a stick pushed into an apple
    Between the green skin and the red.
    Gwenddydd, my darling,
    It now appears to me
    There are so many things I can discern
    That nobody else can see . . .

Why must you wait until he is dead before you make yourself an Emperor?

MEDRAUT (*after a pause*). I was warned against you.

GWENHWYVAR. By Arthur.

MEDRAUT. Not by Arthur.

GWENDDYDD. By Merlin, in point of fact?

MEDRAUT. In point of fact, yes. I was warned that when you met a nobleman you would try to lay waste his honour.

GWENDDYDD. Not the truth.

MEDRAUT. Very much the truth. How dare she put it to me I should usurp the long sword and the red dragon of the battle-standard!

GWENHWYVAR. I did not put it to you.

> It has been in your own mind
> Through the full moon and the hornéd moon
> And the black dark night of the blind.

Besides, you have no honour, there is only the honour of the entire Army – I have heard *that* word often enough among the Companions of Arthur's camp.

> You know that your Roman Army
> Has lost its purpose and its power.
> Lieutenant-General, with this Army
> The coast of the land is not secure.
> Lieutenant-General, you know it well
> For all your beautiful golden head
> That if we are left to the honour of the Army
> We are all of us dishonoured and dead.

MEDRAUT. I have nothing more to say to you. Dylan, where have you gone to! (*He is on his way out, when he stops and turns round again.*) Who, in God's name, is the Daughter of Branwen?

GWENHWYVAR. I am.

MEDRAUT. Oh, you are? And what do you do about it?

GWENHWYVAR. I go into a garden with a fountain in the middle and four white walls of stone all round it, and I begin to play my game – come here and I will show you.

> I make the choice; it is my turn –
> I've chosen you: you are the one!

She presses her thumbnail hard into his forehead.

MEDRAUT. Blood of the Cross, is it the Wild Cats of Galloway who taught you to do that! (*He exits, his hand clapped to his brow.*)

GWENDDYDD. And what happens after that?

GWENHWYVAR. I don't know. It's the first time I have ever played it, you see . . .

GWENDDYDD. Let me look at your thumbnail – you have drawn blood out of his forehead!

GWENHWYVAR. I don't give a fisherman's fart for the honour of his old Army.

> I ask you what kind of Army
> Is he going to have so very soon
> Marked as he is in blood
> With the mark of the hornéd moon?

Exit GWENHWYVAR, *laughing.*
Enter ANEURIN.

ANEURIN. She chose Medraut?

GWENDDYDD. She did.

ANEURIN. Oh God, whatever for?

GWENDDYDD. Would you not call him desirable?

ANEURIN. For himself, or for his rank?

GWENDDYDD.

>His body is white and red
>With here and there a livid scar
>Pale yellow and curled is his hair
>Like the hair of a young ram.
>If he came to me stark naked
>In the middle of a moor
>And he said to me: 'Girl,
>You do not know who I am:
>Will you take me or will you leave me?'
>I don't think I would go away.

ANEURIN.

>There is one reason and one reason alone why the Daughters of Branwen be called home
>There is one reason, it is the same reason, why the battle-standard be broken:
>For how else can I believe that justice will ever be done
>For the men who have lived ever without it, who they are I do not know –
>The very names of their tribes by some conqueror have been imposed,
>Forced under is their ancient language by an alien tongue that will not flow,
>Generation after generation while the long sword has been walking over,
>They have lived and lurked under – altogether without hope
>Except that they have constructed this foolish hope of their own:
>Queen Branwen, they will say to you, once ruled through nothing but love –
>She had need of no General and need of no soldiers

Her lovely land was held in common, no landlord gathered his
  gold,
All of the people ate what all of the people did grow,
And on the day that her huge power once more shall be made
  known
Once more shall the life of the Island of the Mighty
  be exactly as I have told.
Is it probable that Chief Dragon's Lieutenant will be the man to
bring in that power?

GWENDDYDD. What does it matter, if your one hope is such a
foolish one in any case?

ANEURIN. Oh yes, I call it foolish; but remember something else.
  I have been called
  A vagabond and worse
  By those who themselves destroy
  The poetry that they profess.
  I am still here none the less
  I am here: and I make my verse.
So don't be so ready to credit such an easy condemnation. The
power of Branwen can not be brought forward unless the people
themselves demand it. But they cannot demand it unless they
have first seen it, with their own eyes and quite close to them.
And who is to show them this?

GWENDDYDD. Why not yourself, you are a poet?

ANEURIN. Yes, but I can show them nothing till the banner is
broken in two. Who can break it – except Medraut? And upon
whom will be the burden of breaking Medraut in his turn –?

GWENHWYVAR *re-enters. He goes up to her and takes her hands.*

Lady, between your beautiful brown thighs you hold the whole
future of Britain, *enclasped*, like an egg in a cup! You can crack it,
if you want to . . .

GWENHWYVAR. Not yet I can't crack it – there's more work to be
done on him yet. Will you do it for me?

ANEURIN. What is it?

GWENHWYVAR. Just tell him a few answers to the questions he is
likely to ask you. Come, girl, leave him to it.

Exeunt GWENHWYVAR *and* GWENDDYDD. MEDRAUT *enters.
He is deeply disturbed. He has wound his scarf round his brow.*

MEDRAUT. You are said to be a poet. Very different-looking man from Merlin. Learned, are you?

ANEURIN. Observant, I would put it that way.

MEDRAUT. Here is a question. Answer it. I will give you gold. Upon a barren moorland two separate settlements, quite alike, only a river between them. Cattle are kept, sheep, oats and barley, nothing much. The first time you go there you think they are the same people on both sides of the river. But by God you are mistaken. On the left bank they have intercourse with their animals, you are told. On the right bank they eat children. Yet all of them lay claim to be Christian men. How does it happen?

ANEURIN.
For whom do they keep cattle
For whom do they harvest their grain?

MEDRAUT.
For themselves . . ., and for their landlord.

ANEURIN.
Then will not their landlord
Be in fear and in pain
That this year or next year
Themselves and themselves alone
Will take all of the harvest from him
And leave him with none?
So let him make sure
That the river between
Has no bridge built across it:
Let him persuade each of them
That the other one is unclean –
So, there are not enough of them,
At any one time,
To deprive him of his grain.
So, there are not enough of them,
In any one place,
To cut his eyes out of his face
And his heart out of his trunk!
Give me your gold, master –
I will go and get drunk.

MEDRAUT. No, you won't. One more question. Men who have lived for years by fighting against their enemies – stealing cattle, burning houses, making raids by night upon protected sheepfolds –

ANEURIN. Wolves, you might say, not men?

MEDRAUT. Such men, all of a sudden, when called upon to fight against the worst enemy they have ever known, run away into the hills and hide. How does it happen?

Enter DYLAN.

ANEURIN. Ask him.

MEDRAUT. He doesn't know.

ANEURIN. Oh, yes, he does, but perhaps he doesn't know that he knows.

MEDRAUT. Dylan, come here.

DYLAN. Lord –?

MEDRAUT *has for a moment shoved back the scarf from his head.* DYLAN *stares in amazement at the mark made by* GWENHYVAR'S *thumb.*

Lord – what have you put between your eyes, upon your forehead?

MEDRAUT. Mind your business. I have put nothing. I want to ask you –

DYLAN. No, lord – it is the hornéd moon! The Lady Branwen must have put it there – did she come to you in a dream?

MEDRAUT. And why should she come to me? I am a good Christian – are not you?

DYLAN. Oh yes, but the Lady Branwen was alive here for so many years before Christ: we never heard that she was dead – oh, she's not dead, she has *touched* you! The rich man who owns my father's land sent in soldiers once, with a Christian priest, to cut down the grove of trees where my sisters used to dance at festivals. They said terrible things to my sisters, putting the name of whore upon them, yet they are good girls and gentle, and I can tell them from this day that they were quite right in what they did! Lord General –

MEDRAUT. Lieutenant-General –

DYLAN. Lord General! With that mark upon you, you can travel the valleys of Strathclyde and Gododdin, every man will join your Army, every woman will fall at your feet, kiss the corner of your plaid, they will – God, they would get into bed with you if they were not afraid of the anger of the Great Lady –!

ANEURIN. You are made joyful by what you have seen?

DYLAN (*in an ecstasy*). Here is a great lord and a brave soldier who has remembered what every one else of his house has so long forgotten – why should I not be joyful? Bran has come back to us – the Buried Head has risen up – the Princes and the Priests and Conquerors are all of them to be killed! I will go out and tell your soldiers, lord, the whole Island belongs to them all –! (*He rushes out.*)

MEDRAUT. Wait – wait – you can't say that –! Mercy of Heaven, what have you done?

ANEURIN. Me, master? I've done nothing.

Enter STRATHCLYDE.

STRATHCLYDE. I have heard there is the most extraordinary treasonable nonsense being talked within this fort – what do you know about it?

MEDRAUT. Who has talked?

STRATHCLYDE. Among the women.

MEDRAUT. Not my soldiers?

STRATHCLYDE. I don't know about your soldiers – I am talking about the women, all those so-called wives you brought back with you from the cavalry – Pictish heathendom and nothing other, running through them like the bloody flux –

Enter TALIESIN.

TALIESIN. Quite true, my lord – it is a pan full of infected porridge, boiling over. Of course, as a poet I have known it to be simmering for years, but –

STRATHCLYDE. Oh, you have? You didn't tell *me*!

TALIESIN. No, for I ever hoped and believed that our Christian civilization would prove strong enough to keep it under.

STRATHCLYDE. And so it will. Call out my war-band. Gather together all the holy men of God from every church and every hermitage – the name of the Goddess Branwen is not to be spoken in Strathclyde and anyone who dares to –

MEDRAUT. Brother, which is more dangerous? The Goddess Branwen, or the English?

STRATHCLYDE. English – what English? They are not within my realm.

MEDRAUT. No, but they soon will be. And these heretics whom you would destroy are the only ones who can keep them out. Listen to that!

There is a growing turmoil offstage, voices of men and women can be now distinguished shouting: 'Bran lives again, Bran lives again, Bran lives, Bran – Bran – Bran –!'

TALIESIN. Those are not camp-followers. Those are the voices of *your* men.

STRATHCLYDE. Your skirmishers are in a state of mutiny! What the devil will you do now?

MEDRAUT. What can I do but put myself at their head where I belong?

DYLAN erupts on to the stage at the head of a crowd of SKIR-MISHERS and WOMEN – all in a state of frenzy. They carry weapons. The WOMEN are wild-eyed, their hair loose, their behaviour like that of Maenads.

Dylan! Go back to the soldiers – tell them –

DYLAN.
  The mark of the moon is not upon his head
  The servants of Branwen will kill him dead.

He kills STRATHCLYDE, despite MEDRAUT's ineffectual effort to prevent him. Then he turns on TALIESIN.

  Here is a poet who forsook his duty
  He did squat across Our Lady sleeping
  He befouled all her beauty –

ANEURIN. Leave him be, man – he is still a poet! Let him go!

The crowd pauses for an instant, and TALIESIN, his clothes, half-ripped-off and his hair half-pulled-out, is able to make his escape.

DYLAN. We are now going to cut the heads off all the Priests of Christ that we can find.

They all clear rapidly off, dragging the body of STRATHCLYDE by the heels.

MEDRAUT.
  He was my brother
  And he was a buck-toothed bellowing fool.

> Now that I assume my Imperial rule
> May God – or the Goddess – defend
> That I do not behave like him.

Enter GWENHWYVAR.

GWENHWYVAR. This has all happened more quickly than I believed would be possible. (*She appears stunned.*)

MEDRAUT. We are both caught considerably by surprise are we not?

Enter GWENDDYDD.

MEDRAUT. Improvise – we improvise – I have not read the book of Titus Livy, but – (*He grabs* GWENHWYVAR *by the wrist.*)
> You have put your mark upon my brow
> Ha ha – it is my turn now
> To see how many blotches red and thick
> I can imprint on your small scornful neck –

GWENHWYVAR. Wait – there is a ceremony – *wait* –!

MEDRAUT.
> Ceremony – what is that?
> The man who wears a woollen hood
> Does not need to buy a hat!

He hustles her off.

ANEURIN.
> Your woollen hood will cost you far more dear
> Than the widest hat that you could wear
> Let alone a cloth of hair –

GWENDDYDD. She should never have permitted him – not after that tone of voice!

ANEURIN.
> And all he could cry was: 'Beware, beware
> The naked man has come to steal your coat!'

MORGAN enters. She is wearing a fine old cloak of green, embroidered with leaves and flowers – threadbare and dirty indeed, but it covers her rags. She also has a polished white wand instead of her usual bent old stick.

MORGAN. There should have been a ceremony.
> The old man climbs the quaking hill
> One leg well and one leg ill –

He should take his hot bath and ride with his left foot upon the proud stag's backbone, and when he falls off then his leg will have been stretched. And then he would be King – a *lame* King, as is proper, who would obey his Lady in all things. But this one – he is at the head of his wild rogue soldiers, in his hand is a long sword – he does not go to break the Banner of the Dragon: He goes to take it for his own! I tell you he is nothing better than the son of Uther made young. And *she* is aware of it and he wants it to be like that – or she would strangle him upon his bed!

GWENHWYVAR *enters, supported by* MEDRAUT. *She takes a regal stance in the middle of the stage, and he crouches respectfully near her feet. Both of them are wearing special regalia :* GWEN-HWYVAR *has on a leaf-green mantle – a lighter colour than* MORGAN's *– her bare arms emerge through slits in the thick material. She wears a white and silver mask – not a naturalistic face, but formal and regular – by no means grotesque. On the brow of the mask is a silver crescent, the horns pointing upwards.* MEDRAUT *wears a red and green mask of similar pattern with small antlers at the temples. He is naked to the waist and wears a wide collar woven out of ivy and holly leaves.*

GWENHWYVAR (*addressing the audience*). Children of Branwen – your Kingdom is come again!

A great noise of music and shouting. Thunder and lightning. MEDRAUT *suddenly leaps to his feet and comes downstage of* GWENHWYVAR.

MEDRAUT. And I am the Emperor of it!

DYLAN *runs in carrying a naked sword. He throws this to* MEDRAUT *who catches it deftly and brandishes it. The noise increases, becoming a continuous roar ; and then stops.*

I intend to be acknowledged Emperor by all the men of the Christian Army and perhaps even by that butcher of his own blood who still calls himself Chief Dragon.

DYLAN *walks round the stage, exhorting, with gestures, an unseen multitude. Cheers and shouts, as before – 'Bran lives again', etc.*

The Island of the Mighty belongs to us, it belongs to all of us, it belongs to the Children of Branwen – and we shall never let it go!

The cheers continue and are merged into triumphant music. MEDRAUT *and* DYLAN *dance around the stage, leaping and prancing like excited deer.* GWENHWYVAR *remains still where she is, her body has swayed and drooped, and her masked face has fallen over sideways.* GWENDDYDD, MORGAN *and* ANEURIN *are at one side, on the forestage.*

GWENDDYDD. Butcher of his own blood? Exactly why did he say that?

MORGAN. Because that is what Arthur son of Uther has been . . . it's what he *is* . . . he always will be . . . But *this* one only knows it because I was fool enough to tell him so . . .

She tears off her green cloak and rips it in shreds. At every rip she spits on the ground.

Spit: He is forgotten. Spit: He never lived. Spit: We are all fools and the world is as it ever was . . .

MEDRAUT *concludes his parading around and returns to* GWEN-HWYVAR. *She does not appear to realize he is there. He takes her by the hand to lead her off but she sways and seems about to fall.* DYLAN *takes her other elbow, and between them she is brought off the stage, her feet stumbling.* MORGAN *follows them at a distance, still tearing the material of her cloak.*

ANEURIN. I will go to Arthur's camp and talk to Merlin. Merlin is no good, but he has a head upon his shoulders. You had better come with me – there is nothing you can do in Carlisle. It all happened so quickly, you see. We never understood what it was we had to do. No more did Gwenhwyvar. Playing games with it – games – a little girl, and dirty, within the shelter of a four-walled garden!

GWENDDYDD. Strangle him, said Morgan, strangle him upon the bed. She might do it yet.

ANEURIN (*shaking his head*). I ought to have stayed behind and set myself to work against him. But when the swords are out, I am a coward.

SCENE TEN

Camp.

ANEURIN *and* GWENDDYDD *have been walking round the stage.
Now they stop.*

ANEURIN. Observe. We are forestalled. A gentleman is here before
us.

Enter TALIESIN.

TALIESIN. You saved my life.
ANEURIN. Would you have saved mine? Unless Medraut's men
rise up against him, which I doubt, he will soon have them
slaughtering all the poets everywhere. Because even bad poets,
Taliesin, will know that Medraut does not talk truth. It will take
quite a long time for the people to discover that.
GWENDDYDD. Oh, they will discover it. You and I have not
sharper brains than anyone else. We are better informed, that is
all.

Enter MERLIN.

MERLIN. Better informed, and yet you have done this.
ANEURIN. Me? I've done nothing.
MERLIN. You have made verses! Do you dare to call that nothing!
You had better tell me exactly what is happening in Carlisle.
ANEURIN. He has augmented his army. He has added to his own
men the warband of Strathclyde and several hundred Picts out of
the mountains of Galloway. He is about to march upon Arthur's
squadrons to claim their obedience, or else to destroy them –
whichever comes first.
MERLIN. Then we must destroy *him*. There is no possible alterna-
tive. Is it true he has come to an agreement with the English?
ANEURIN. He has kept very silent about the English.
MERLIN. Medraut is now a heathen: the English are heathen.
Why should they not agree?

Enter BEDWYR *in his war-gear.*

BEDWYR. Have you spoken upon this to the General, Chief Poet?

MERLIN. I have not.

BEDWYR. Not an easy matter to bring such a word to such a man. I have made an attempt at it. That lame leg of his – almost unable to move it at all now – why, look you – it takes two men to help him walk across the camp, though he will not let them touch him.

> ARTHUR *comes in. Two* COMPANIONS *are with him, in case he falls – they are in their war-gear.* ARTHUR *is half-dressed in his Imperial Roman parade-uniform (as seen in Part One, Scene Three). He is dragging the dragon-standard with him, clumsily, and trying to wrench away the skull.*

Chief Dragon – the battle-standard – let me take it, you will damage it – what is he doing, for God's sake?

ARTHUR. Cain has killed Abel. And we know who he is because of the mark upon his brow. I have a mark upon *my* brow – do you know how it was caused?

BEDWYR. Cut of a Saxon blade upon the slope of Badon Hill. I was there, I saw it happen.

ARTHUR. And did you see what was *here* before you saw it happen?
Beneath the long love-lock I used to wear
Of youthful yellow curling hair.

I knew Strathclyde was dead, I had a dream of him last night. He was running along the top of Caesar's Wall and shouting for me. He was calling out that his mother wanted me – he seemed to be no more than four or five years old. I attempted to tell him that his mother was no longer alive and therefore I could not go to her – but I was unable to get out of my bed. Why was that? The red dragon had taken me by the throat. . . . Cain, did I say Cain, his name is not Cain, his name is Bran the Blessed, he is the Defender of the Island, do they all desert me and run to him because of it? Old soldier, will you run?

FIRST COMPANION. I will not.

ARTHUR. No, you had better not. If you did, in short order you would be most sorely disillusioned. Bran the Blessed, do you know, was a most mighty hero – yes – but he is *not* in Carlisle –

MERLIN. General – not appropriate!

ARTHUR. Shut your mouth. You are a poet, you have done nothing to contradict the enormous falsehoods that have been told! Companions, here is truth: he is *not* in Carlisle.

With an effort he succeeds in removing the skull from the standard.
He holds it in his hand and shows it to them.

Quite a small man he must have been
My fingers go right round his face
And see, his teeth stick out between . . .

A pause.

SECOND COMPANION. And he has hung upon your banner for how
long?

BEDWYR. For more than twenty years. And through that time young
Medraut has grown up out of nothing.
While he has become stronger
And more beautiful every day
All our good fortune
Has withered away.

FIRST COMPANION.
And I know exactly
When that withering began.

SECOND COMPANION.
The hour you put the nail
Through the dead-white bone of Bran.

ARTHUR.
I had thought it would encourage them
To show them what I had done . . .
No good, no good at all. Throw it away, boy, get rid of it quickly.

He throws the skull to ANEURIN *who tosses it off the stage.*

BEDWYR. Look, your cloak is falling off, let me fasten it up for
you . . .

ARTHUR. Are you a Captain of Horse or a dribbling nursemaid? No
no, I am collapsing – I have an ague, Bedwyr . . . my faculties are
gone.

GWENDDYDD. Tell me why Medraut has called you a butcher of
your blood.

ARTHUR. Strumpet, sorceress, cannibal of men's flesh, you are a
cavern full of pox and pus – very well you know the answer –!

GWENDDYDD. I swear to you I do not.

ARTHUR. Somebody fasten my cloak for me – I can't manage it – my fingers . . . I have an old filthy sister, her name is Morgan, she is mad. There is nobody but herself could have told my wife to do this to me – am I right, girl?

GWENDDYDD. I won't gainsay you.

ARTHUR. I had another sister once, she was the wife of the Prince of Strathclyde, and she had three sons. Useless idiots. Then she had a fourth. He was not useless. His name was Medraut. It so happened that he was *my* son. Yes, my own sister had me creep into her bed, because Morgan told us it was needful – for the security of the land. The wife of Strathclyde was the Daughter of Branwen, you see – I was marked upon my head, I was made lame by a strange ceremony. But by God I was a Christian and I knew at once I had done wrong. I remembered Constantine Emperor: he saw a sign in the sky, it was a Cross and he did conquer. I remembered Maximus Emperor, he lay with the Daughter of Branwen, and he was defeated. So I kept it all so secret, I killed everyone who knew anything. Except of course for Morgan – up hill and down dale I went searching for her. I never found her at all. But I came back and killed my sister, who was my wife. She was drowned, as it were by accident, as she crossed over a flooded ford; and the child that was wrapped up in her shawl, which was my child, was intended to be drowned as well. And he was not. He was hauled out of the millrace by the miller of Carlisle, and I looked at him – they were all running, they cried, 'Tragedy, the lady's dead!' I looked at him, he was a child. I could not kill him after that. So I brought him up to be my officer, my successor in due course; in due course is now today . . . Oh God help me, go and join yourselves with Medraut, I am shaking all to pieces, there is nothing left of me at all . . .

BEDWYR. Now listen to me, General. We are Companions, we are your men! Our defences are wide open between here and the Strathclyde border. If he comes at us directly we shall not stand a chance. General, will you not tell us what we are going to do – *now*!

THE COMPANIONS. You must tell us – we must have orders – the whole Army is in confusion –

ARTHUR. Do –? What else to do –? We are an Army – we must fight – that is all that we know about – *fight*.

FIRST COMPANION. We can't fight him from here – not from this position –

SECOND COMPANION. Didn't you hear us – we are wide open –

ARTHUR. Then we march to the west and we meet him as he comes.

MERLIN. And who will come after us?

BEDWYR. Yes, General, the English, they are bound to take advantage.

ARTHUR. Your job is to prevent them. I give you command of the rear-guard, Bedwyr – two whole squadrons in your new fort toward the south.

BEDWYR. And who will command the main body?

ARTHUR. Should there be any doubt about that?

BEDWYR. You are not fit.

ARTHUR. So says Medraut. Are you with him or against him? Bedwyr, who is the General?

BEDWYR. You.

ARTHUR. And it will be the General who carries his own red dragon into battle. Not appropriate to leave the standard with the commander of the rear-guard – *my* hand – for *this* engagement.

ARTHUR *and the* SOLDIERS *go out.*

TALIESIN. Merlin, this must be stopped. Medraut is his own son.

MERLIN. Medraut is an apostate.

TALIESIN. They must be brought together and made friends.

MERLIN. Not at all. Not at all. They are determined upon death.

TALIESIN. The highest function of our traditional craft is the mediation of peace. We must walk between the armies and persuade them by our rhetoric.

MERLIN. After what we have just heard? No, Taliesin.

First: Medraut dead.

Then the English: all dead.

Then let Arthur roll himself up

And tumble alone into his frozen bed.

It is not possible that I shall survive him. Therefore come with me, wife, come with me to my tent.

He goes out. GWENDDYDD, *with the briefest possible pause for reflection, goes out with him.* TALIESIN *goes out separately.*

SCENE ELEVEN

Woodland.

ARTHUR *enters slowly, leaning on the dragon-banner, which has been damaged by swordcuts. He is fully clad in his parade-armour, the vizor-mask of his helmet closed. He is badly wounded and blood seeps out from under the helmet across the top of his cuirass. He carries his sword and it is broken.*

ANEURIN. The highest function of our traditional craft – not for the first time – failed. Medraut led his Army out of Carlisle and marched east. Arthur marched west. The place where they met was called Camlann – a ruined gateway on the Roman Wall, where once a road had led northward out of the civil land into the wild. It was pouring with rain and Arthur's great horses sank deep into the boggy ground. Nevertheless the old men who bestrode them were very difficult to kill. Then the English, as expected, came up behind, they were fighting with Bedwyr and they drove him hard, on into the main battle. It was the first great defeat Arthur had ever had, but Medraut was defeated too. The English attacked both of them, murdering all the Welshmen on either side, without mercy. Then they returned to their stockades and waited for the spring, for their wives and their children to come over from Germany. What happened to Medraut?

> BEDWYR *enters, wounded. He tries to help* ARTHUR.

ARTHUR. Medraut is dead . . .

> *He drops his broken sword,* BEDWYR *picks it up and hands it back to him.* ARTHUR *refuses to take it.*

Let nobody again ever have hold of it, Bedwyr . . .

> ARTHUR *drags painfully at his vizor which is distorted and hard to open. He opens it and takes off the helmet. His face is covered with blood.*

Throw it away – I said throw the sword away – into deep water – anywhere. Drown it. Forget it. And *this* can go with it.

He breaks the pole of the dragon-standard in two and flings the pieces to the ground.

Another twenty years and no one will know what the dragon was ever for, who carried it, how it died . . . Medraut is dead . . .

BEDWYR. You told me. You are not dead.

ARTHUR (*failing fast*). Yes . . . No grave . . . Dig no grave, Bedwyr . . . not wise, a grave for Arthur. Who knows who might not come to it and dig up my head . . . ? I am not the Brother of Branwen. *Imperator non sum.*

He lurches out, BEDWYR *after him, leaving the broken banner and his helmet behind him.*

ANEURIN. What happened to Gwenhwyvar?
    A blood-stained Englishman, I have been told,
    Fell in with her upon the bloodstained field.
    He took her and he dragged her with a rope
    Into a wood convenient for rape.
    And afterwards, he felt some sort of love,
    He tended her and made her his own slave.
    She cooked his food and kept his house-place clean.
    Quite quiet they lived and she did not complain.
Yet the man has a wife already – across the sea, I wouldn't wonder . . . will she never learn anything? What happened to Merlin? Lord of historical wisdom, creator of virtuous verse, he craved for destruction and he is himself destroyed. Not his body, which was always feeble, but his mind, for which alone he claimed to live.

MERLIN *enters, his clothes thrown off, his eyes wild.*

MERLIN. Merlin is a bird! Merlin grows feathers! Merlin will fly everywhere . . .

Exeunt.

THE ISLAND OF
THE MIGHTY

Part Three

A HANDFUL OF WATERCRESS

Concerning Merlin –
how he needed to be alone
and then
how he needed not to be alone

SCENE ONE

Raid.

ANEURIN (*enters, singing*).
    So Arthur is dead and Medraut dead
    Upon the field they call Camlann.
    This is the tale of one who lived
    And ran stark crazy in his pain.
    It has been said that the death he saw
    And the blood he smelt and the cries he heard
    Struck him so deep at his brain-root
    What could he do but become a bird?

    MERLIN *enters, dressed as at the end of Part Two, in his drawers or breechclout, nothing else. He sits down in a corner and huddles himself in his arms, shivering and squeaking slightly.*

MERLIN. Merlin is a bird. Merlin has feathers. Merlin will fly everywhere.

    Enter GWENDDYDD, *in front.*

GWENDDYDD. There was more to it than that, though.

ANEURIN. Yes, he could have prevented the battle altogether. He was an established celebrated bard and he believed most fervently in the power of his ordered profession. According to his own rule he should have worked until death through his words and his music to reconcile the great commanders. He did not even try.

GWENDDYDD. Aneurin Poet, that is not just. You yourself made no attempt –

ANEURIN. Did not want to. Would not have been accepted if I had. Never desired to be accepted by the men of the long sword. But Merlin did and Merlin was. Good God, he was your husband, you know it better than anyone. Why the night before the battle he took you with him to his tent. Not to discourse upon love, I dare well hazard.

GWENDDYDD. Indeed not. Rather to discourse upon the duty of a poet when great commanders are at enmity . . .

MERLIN *gets up, picks up a blanket from the corner of the stage, wraps himself in it, and strides up and down in an agitated manner.*

GWENDDYDD. Oh God, what a conversation. He did not approach within six feet of me all night, and yet it was he that had invited me in . . .

The tinkling of the bells on TALIESIN'S *staff are heard offstage.*

MERLIN. Oh yes, you hear that noise, Gwenddydd – do you know what it is? Yes, do you know what it is? It is Taliesin Chief Poet. He walks backwards and forwards all night between Medraut's camp and this one, beseeching each commander to listen to his proposals for a negotiated truce. He will not produce agreement.

GWENDDYDD. If you were to help him perhaps he could.

MERLIN. Oh no.

TALIESIN (*off*). Merlin!

MERLIN. Oh no.

TALIESIN *enters in his official dress.*

TALIESIN. I have spoken to them both. As I feared, they are quite obdurate.

MERLIN. I told you that they would be.

TALIESIN. So what is to be done?

MERLIN. Arthur must win his battle. The Christian Army must prevail. That is what is to be done.

TALIESIN. But the soldiers of Medraut are nearly all of them Christian if only they could be brought back to it. They have been abominably misled. One voice they could respect – your voice – there is no other. Merlin, you *must* help me!

MERLIN. Help you, man? To the camp of Medraut, do you mean, and bleat like a sheep to his soldiers? Why, he would kill me the minute he sees me. I am surprised he has not killed you. He tried to, in Carlisle.

TALIESIN. On that occasion I was not dressed in the sacred robe of my office.

MERLIN. Neither am I on this occasion. It has amazingly escaped your notice, Taliesin, but there is a young woman in this tent. She is my wife. I wish to lie with her. Will you leave us in private?

TALIESIN.

> Then what I must do
> I must do upon my own.
> I am an old man and by no means full of valour.
> But tomorrow morning, you,
> In your prime of life, you will be shown
> That an old man knows his duty,
> Despite the shaking pallor
> Of his face and the intermittent groan
> Of his overloaded belly,
> Yes and the creaking of each bone --
> Oh I have known
> All the jeers you have passed on me and your intellectual
> scorn.
> You are welcome to your wife.
> So many years since last she was yours --
> May you enjoy her all your life. (*Exit.*)

GWENDDYDD. Do you wish to? You don't deserve it. But you see, I did come in.

MERLIN.

> On the roof of the tent
> I hear drops of dark rain.
> Arthur's horses cannot fight
> If the moorland ground is soft and wet.
> What tactic do you think
> He will be able to think out?

GWENDDYDD.

> If you really believe what you told Taliesin
> You would take yourself off to the tent of your General
> And there you would inspire him to a tactic without parallel --
> Just a song and a verse and an old tale out of British history
> And you would be the Poet of his Thirteenth Great Victory.
> So why don't you go, then? Quite clear you don't want *me*.

MERLIN. Oh God, oh God, oh God -- how can I inspire any man to take up the sword against his own flesh and blood! Don't you see, I can't do anything!

GWENDDYDD. And neither can I. So go to sleep and don't be frightened. When all's said, you yourself do not have to fight in the battle. I will sing you to sleep -- husband.

MERLIN *huddles up in his blanket and tries to sleep.* GWEND-
DYDD *crouches a little way from him and sings – in a manner
hardly suited to a lullaby, being more of a keen. She sings:*

Oh the ravens
There is no pleasure but for the black ravens
Oh the ravens
Tomorrow they are going to eat
Oh the ravens
There is no pleasure but for the black ravens
Oh the ravens
Tonight they do not want to sleep
Oh the ravens
There is no pleasure but for the black ravens
Oh the ravens
There will be blood on their claws and their beaks . . .

ANEURIN (*on the forestage, his cloak pulled over his head*). I was
myself situated that night beneath a little tree beside the camp and
I had no shelter against the rain. So I found myself singing the
same song as she did – it is very old and very hopeless and no one
knows who made it –

GWENDDYDD *goes on singing and he joins in.*

GWENDDYDD *and* ANEURIN (*singing*).
Oh the ravens
There is no pleasure but for the black ravens
Oh the ravens
Tomorrow they will tear at their meat
Oh the ravens
There is no pleasure but for the black ravens
Oh the ravens
Their victory will be complete . . .

SCENE TWO

Woodland

Enter TALIESIN, *upstage.*

TALIESIN. I am Taliesin Chief Poet and I claim recognition of my sacred status upon this field! Let no man draw his weapon for as long as I stand here, robed, with my rod of office in my hand. Between the embattled hosts of Britain I do solemnly declare this war to be Fratricidal, Parricidal, Internecine, and most Blasphemous!

MERLIN. He's gone mad. He goes and stands there in the pouring rain wet as a washcloth, and he thinks he can *forbid* the battle! He does believe that in this day and age there are warriors in Britain who will veritably respect the Authority of a Poet?

GWENDDYDD. No, they will doubtless hoot at him, perhaps they will throw stones. Are they doing so already – what *are* they doing, Merlin?

MERLIN (*amazed*). In complete silence they stand still . . . and they listen to what he says . . . ?

> TALIESIN *climbs up one of the posts at the side of the stage and looks from side to side, slowly. Then he starts to chant, emphasizing the rhythm of his words by shaking his stick with its bells.*

TALIESIN (*chanting*).
Flint put up and bronze put down
Hand unclench from heft of bone
Horses loose beneath the yoke
Helmet-strap no longer choke.

MERLIN. You know what he is saying, don't you? The most ancient words of all for this particular function of the Poet – oh, they cannot have been made use of since the men of Britain fought from chariots.

TALIESIN (*chanting*).
Bronze put down and flint put up
Helmet turn into a cup
Fill with wine and pour it out
First to the earth and then to the throat.

MERLIN. I thought I was the only Bard alive who had memory of this jargon – and yet I have never spoken it – while *he* – upon the moor of Camlann, over against the very gap of my tent – he presents himself as blatant as the balls of a bull, and he shouts it aloud with pride! My God, he has been rummaging in my tent among my documents!

TALIESIN (*chanting*).

> Shield and cloak on ground be spread
> Sit down and drink and cool your head
> Shield and cloak on ground be spread
> Sit down and drink and cool your head.
> By word of Poet this battle is forbid!

He jumps down and strikes about the stage repeating his last line forcibly as though addressing masses of men in different directions.

MERLIN.

> By word of Poet my General is betrayed
> His twelve great victories are all betrayed
> The lives of his brave Companions are every one of them betrayed
> The English will grip everything –!

I am going out to him, now! I am going to shut up his mouth!

GWENDDYDD. You will lay your hand upon a *Poet* –?

MERLIN. Not my *hand* – no –

He runs out and returns immediately with a short spear. GWEND-DYDD *tries to stop him – she grabs at the blanket he wears but he shakes himself free and runs upstage to* TALIESIN, *leaving the blanket behind in her hand.*

MERLIN (*to* TALIESIN). I do desire you should give over this anachronistic provocation. You do not enhance the dignity of –

TALIESIN. Merlin – I think I've done it – the two armies have stood stock still!

MERLIN. Impossible to achieve anything but make our honourable craft into a laughing-stock! You old fool, clear off out of it, and let my General set forward his banner!

TALIESIN. I will not, and you can't compel me.

MERLIN. Yes.

He runs his spear into TALIESIN, *who staggers, falls, and pulls himself slowly up on to his feet again by using his staff. He rocks, and the bells on the staff tinkle.*

TALIESIN. My curse upon you, Merlin, for what you have done. Even as you ran, naked, from your tent, to shed the blood of a fellow-poet, so shall you run naked for the rest of your life. Wild and erratic as flew your spear against my body, so like a wild bird shall you fly at random among the tree-tops, and so shall you come to your end, at the point of a spear.

MERLIN *is standing in a state of shock.* GWENDYDD *comes up and puts the blanket over his shoulders.*

Gwenddydd, wife of Merlin, no curse upon you, girl. For your hand was on his garment to hold him back, and great happiness at the end shall be held back and kept for you. Insofar as it is possible for a woman of such wantonness ever to be happy . . .

He staggers again.

If someone does not come and help me I am going to die of this wound.

He looks all round for help. GWENDDYDD *puts out her hand to him but he ignores it and stumbles off the stage, leaning heavily on his staff.*

ANEURIN (*singing*).
There was no help for him, no help
For any man upon that moor:
Nothing was left but to put breath
Into the roaring horns of war.
Upon both sides the soldiers took
One stride, then two, and then a third.
At every stride they did let fly
The loudest cry that ever was heard –

He cries three times, reinforced by the music.

MERLIN. There was I, there, in the middle of the field, and it was there that I heard them shout. Not alone their shouts did I hear, but the echo and reverberation after in the clouds of heaven and in the vault of the firmament. And I cast my eyes upward, not understanding why the terrible noise should continue so long. Above me there were all these birds, I suppose ravens – it could not be the ravens who were roaring with such persistence? Not be the ravens alone who were filling me with all this turbulence and darkness, and fury, and giddiness, and frenzy, and flight, unsteadiness and restlessness, unquiet, disgust – disgust –?

GWENDDYDD. Disgust with every place in which he used to be and desire for every place he had not yet reached.

ANEURIN (*singing*).

> And from that field he whirled and went
> Before one drop of blood was shed
> Before one sword had cut red meat
> It was not as a man he fled.

MERLIN *spins round, throws off the blanket, drops the spear, and runs round and round and out, crying as he goes.*

Merlin – is – a – bird . . . !

GWENDDYDD *picks up the spear and the blanket and stands staring after him, her mouth open and a moan of terror coming out of it. Exit.*

ANEURIN (*singing*).

> How very few there were who fought
> In Camlann battle and survived.
> Grey-haired Bedwyr was one of them
> And he has seen his General die.

BEDWYR *and some* COMPANIONS *enter, exhausted and wounded.* BEDWYR *is holding* ARTHUR'S *broken sword.*

BEDWYR. I saw him die.

SECOND COMPANION. Appropriate we should go back there and look for his body? Bury it?

BEDWYR. Not wise. English heathen. Everywhere killing. Kill you. They will kill me.

FIRST COMPANION. Oh, but I killed *them*. Scores of them. Yes.

SECOND COMPANION. They will not attack further. They will go back to their camp. Why don't we go back to ours?

THIRD COMPANION. Where is it?

SECOND COMPANION. Carlisle? It is a fort. It will be empty. Medraut is destroyed as well as us. We ought to go there.

THIRD COMPANION. Not enough of us left to make a garrison, I think. Bedwyr, what do *you* think?

BEDWYR. I saw him die.

MERLIN'S VOICE.

> I saw him die
> With my little eye
> I was flying so high
> Look at me and watch me fly.

They look around for him and at last see his face up above them,
behind – he is up among the shadows at the back of the stage. Then
he disappears.

THIRD COMPANION. That was a man?

SECOND COMPANION. If it was a bird, it was a bird that knows
   how to talk in metre and rhyme.

THIRD COMPANION. Moreover, it was a bird as big as a full-
   grown sheep.

FIRST COMPANION. I think it was a ghost.

BEDWYR. Whose ghost?

FIRST COMPANION. Taliesin. He was a poet; he was killed.

SECOND COMPANION. No. Spitted, but not dead.

BEDWYR. And if he was, he would be dead with honour, therefore
   he would leave no ghost. Merlin has no honour for what he
   has done; and he is not dead. *That* was Merlin. Companions, we
   are not permitted by the rules of our trade to have pity for ourselves. But we must pity him, for he broke the rules of *his*
   trade, which are far harder to keep than ours. It is possible he can
   be rescued. Something, in all of Britain, from today's bad work,
   can surely be rescued . . . ? Get after him – Merlin? Chief Poet!
   Do not be afraid, we are the Companions of Arthur. Chief Poet,
   we are your friends –!

FIRST COMPANION. No – no – he has gone from us. Come, wrap
   yourself up, man – we have our own lives to look after . . .

BEDWYR. Carlisle.

ANEURIN (*singing*).

   In Carlisle fort one thousand rats
   Creep in and out quite unafraid –
   The dogs are gone, for the men are dead
   By whom those hungry dogs were fed . . .

SCENE THREE

Fort.

BEDWYR (*suddenly*). There is a rat – go get him –

COMPANIONS (*all hunting*). Catch him – corner him – there he is – etc....

BEDWYR. No, no, he's gone from us. Direct down into his hole. Leave him be and come back to me ... No possibility any longer to garrison this place and defend it. Must make use of it only as a temporary staging-post, gather together what few stragglers yet remain to come in to us and then perhaps move south again to our old headquarters at Caerleon. I could assume command. Would you continue to serve? You would follow me, would you, as though I were Arthur? Arthur had nothing better when he recruited me.

FIRST COMPANION. Oh yes he had – he had hope.

BEDWYR. Hope? Hope went crazy – with Merlin. He was the voice of the General. He was the good fortune of the Island. Even more so than the Head of Bran. Never can you find warriors that will fight without a poet to make it known for what reason they should muster.

> *Enter* TALIESIN, *swathed in filthy bandages, hobbling on a crutch.*

SECOND COMPANION (*indicating* TALIESIN). Ho – but we've got one!

TALIESIN.

> God alone can give you hope.
> God was asleep
> Then He awoke
> He heard how Arthur spoke
> And He helped him heave his spear
> That put the heathen men to fear.
> Then He saw what Arthur did,
> When weary of interminable war
> He rolled and grunted on the bed
> Where spread her legs and blew her wind
> That reeking whore
> Called Blasphemy, Apostasy,
> Despair of heart and mind –

BEDWYR. You speak not from your mouth but from the wound that Merlin gave you – bloody tongue of foul green gangrene – no purpose in it – be quiet!

TALIESIN.
> God's heart and mind
> Towards his wicked people
> Are no longer kind.
> He is no longer sleeping. He has sent
> Full wakefully His righteous chastisement.

He goes out, groaning with pain.

BEDWYR (*suddenly*). Look out, man, there it comes again – kill it, go hunt it – ya-hoo . . . !

Rat-hunt again – this time it brings them all in a body on to the forestage where they all fall over ANEURIN.

FIRST COMPANION. Get out of it –

BEDWYR. Wait –

SECOND COMPANION (*grabbing* ANEURIN). Caught one!

BEDWYR. Come here.

SECOND COMPANION. Here he is. He is a poet.

ANEURIN. After a fashion.

BEDWYR. Rat-fashion. Yes. But a poet none the less. Where is the girl?

ANEURIN. What girl?

BEDWYR. The wife of Merlin. Don't pretend you don't know. You came into Carlisle with her. By God, I saw you at the gate. You are keeping her, are you, till her husband returns to claim her – or *what* are you doing with her, indecent that you are?

ANEURIN. I'm doing nothing at all with her, except to preserve her from harm and to see that she does not starve.

BEDWYR. Perhaps true. Perhaps not true. At all events, go call her here.

ANEURIN. Call –?

BEDWYR. You are not deaf, are you, as well as dirty? I said to call her here.

ANEURIN. Very well then. Gwenddydd!

Enter GWENDDYDD.

GWENDDYDD. You called my name?

ANEURIN. Somebody told me to call it.

BEDWYR. So listen to me, both of you. The man Merlin is out of his mind. If he were not out of his mind he could be of great use to me – here. You need not ask me what use – I say he could be of use. Now, in my belief, his madness has been an act of his own will.

GWENDDYDD. His own will? He has been cursed by a fellow-poet to whom he did a blood-injury.

ANEURIN. And Merlin knows well enough that that curse must take effect. He would be false to his own trade if he endeavoured to fight against it.

GWENDDYDD. Oh, false he has long been indeed; but not *that* false, I can tell you.

BEDWYR. So you confirm me what I said. Entirely of his own will. He has permitted it – he has *submitted* to the curse. Look at me – I am sane enough, you will agree – you will agree – you will agree –!

His voice has risen alarmingly and he glares around at his COMPANIONS.

COMPANIONS (*nervously*). Agreed – agreed – Captain . . .

BEDWYR. I should hope so! You get out of it! This is not for your ears – we discuss the craft of poetry, which is for Princes and great men. Out!

Disturbed, the COMPANIONS *go out.*

I was not a great man; but I saw my General die. At that time I knew inside me that I too could go mad. But I determined to the contrary. Therefore I tell you that Merlin also can determine to the contrary. So who is to help him do it? You were his wife.

GWENDDYDD. For years I had not lived with him. I know so little about him. I don't think I can help him.

BEDWYR. Perhaps true – perhaps not true . . . Then what about you?

ANEURIN. Not me indeed.

BEDWYR. Not?

ANEURIN.
You may think it took him but a moment
To put out his hand and drive that spear.
Great error. He had been in the doing of it
Year after year after year after year –
Driving his barb, you see, into his wife
And into himself and into his poetry –

He has done nothing else for the whole of his life
And now that he has discovered
Upon what road it was he staggered
There is no one can turn him off it:
He must thread his own way home again
Through thorns and bog and snow and rain,
He must put his bleeding feet
One by one where they did tread before
Until he comes once more
Upon the doorstep of the door
From which so long ago he strutted out –
God damn him, what a surprise for him,
He is going to find it shut!

GWENDDYDD. By Christ you are too cruel!

ANEURIN. Cruel? No, I tell truth.

GWENDDYDD. He must be brought back –

BEDWYR. Aha –

GWENDDYDD. He is alone out there, without food – frozen –

BEDWYR (*indicates* ANEURIN). So persuade him. *He* must do it. *He* is a poet. *He* knows the way.

GWENDDYDD. But I will not have Merlin *compelled*. If that is the only manner we can find to bring him back, then I shall not permit it.

BEDWYR. So persuade *him*. Persuade him to persuade Merlin. *He* must do it. *Him*. Take him out for a walk and talk to him. (*Exit.*)

SCENE FOUR

Seascape.

ANEURIN. So many years you have not lived with Merlin, and now you want him? I don't believe it. All he ever was was a poet for men like Arthur – or Bedwyr – what, the very word that has just been given us – for Princes and great men? Taliesin was another of them. And so they curse and hurt each other. What is that? To you and me – quite nothing.

GWENDDYDD. Yes, cruel, but you tell truth. And yet there was a time when I would have said it was not true at all . . . I could not have seen him then more than two, three, four occasions. And then only in the company of a crowd of other people. I had better tell you how it was –

My father was a little Prince. He ruled over a few miles of marshland south of the River Trent, what they call the Fen Country. He paid a regular tribute for the protection of Arthur's Army. And so Merlin would come to visit us, to collect the tribute and to hold talk with my father about matters of state. After dinner he would sing his songs. I did not care for Merlin's verses – which were all of war and potent ancestors: there was his music that went with the verses – in the middle of it he would hood his eyes and look out at me sideways across the strings of his harp. He was so dark and sharp and rapid, his voice became a meaning-less rainstorm upon a wooden roof, it was as though he had crept under the table and groped up at me in secret. I was, you see, no more than thirteen or fourteen, I was ungroped-at altogether, as well-protected by my father as Arthur protected him. I didn't know what was happening that I shifted and shifted upon the hot bench from one cheek to the other: 'Oh my goodness', I would say to my sister – 'What a tedious poet – why don't he stop?' – I would grip her hand till the nails dug in. And then it happened upon one day in a corner of the fen, I was sitting under the sun-shine quite surrounded by bulrushes, all alone and unobserved – or so I thought. Until his face came through the bulrushes at a height of two feet from the ground. I was frightened; but he screwed up his nostrils, put his finger to his lips, shut one eye and laughed. Then he fell over into a puddle, and we both laughed. 'Songs,' he said. 'Songs of war – so tedious to a young girl. I have other music also.' And he began to sing to me directly. (*She sings.*)

> Between the willow and the water
> I found the King's Daughter
> Washing her feet
> And washing her thighs
> Washing her body
> Right up to her eyes –

ANEURIN (*singing*).

> I said to her: 'King's Daughter
> There is nothing I can offer –

I once had a cloak
Of red leather and gold
But a Beggarman went and stole it
When the weather was wet and cold –
I once had a collar of silver
That did gleam like a running river
But a boisterous greedy Captain
Snatched it into his hand
He was jealous of my finery
That I should look so grand –
I once had a long silk kerchief
Embroidered with flowers of purple
But I gave it to the Priest
For forgiveness of my sin
He took it and he folded it
Three times around his chin.'
Oh, I hoped to gain her affection
By telling of my affliction
Of how I had been robbed.
But she tore off my coat
And she hit me with a stick
And she bit me in the throat.

GWENDDYDD. God help us, for what reason would she do a thing
like that?

ANEURIN (*singing*).
'The strongest robber in all this land,'
She cried as she smote me with her hand,
'Is not so proud as to refuse to offer
Half his booty to the tall King's
Daughter –'

ANEURIN *and* GWENDDYDD (*singing together*).
'I have your collar and I have your cloak
And I have your kerchief made of silk.'

GWENDDYDD (*singing*).
'If I'd wanted you, three men or four
Would have grabbed you and thrown you into my door!'

ANEURIN. That song was never made by Merlin.

GWENDDYDD. Indeed it was.

ANEURIN. But you yourself have sung it – many times – I've heard
you – that's how I came to know it.

GWENDDYDD. I did not sing it chiefly because it was his. Rather it was a song that for the first time told me what kind of a woman I wanted to become. Not that I ever did, of course – but upon that day among the bulrushes, where before his music had groped at me, now his *words* and his music thrusted and lunged: and he himself, without his music. Without his trousers, if it comes to that. God, so much mud there was afterwards upon my gown and the bare backs of my legs – had my father detected it, he would have murdered that poet. But he didn't; and in due course, with due permission and a proper contract, I became married to Master Merlin.

ANEURIN. He sang to you again like that, did he, after you were married?

GWENDDYDD. For a time he did, yes. Then bit by bit he forgot about it.

ANEURIN. How many songs of that nature had he made?

GWENDDYDD. Scores of them.

ANEURIN. He was already Chief Poet when he composed them?

GWENDDYDD. Oh yes. But later on he gave them up. He said they were not relevant.

ANEURIN. And did you ask him what *was* relevant?

GWENDDYDD. I put the question. Once. I got an answer. He ground it through closed teeth with his head twisted under his elbow. He said: 'It is the chiefest problem of our age, girl, the most crucial question of them all. Why is it that Jesus Christ has not come back to us, when He did make promise that he would?' I was washing his dirty shirt for him in the yard of our house. As soon as I heard what he said, I dropped the shirt upon the flag-stones, pulled my plaid around my head, and ran out into the road. There was an Irish horsecoper passing by; he had come to sell remounts in the camp of the Army. He made a face at me and clicked his tongue, so I jumped up on his horse behind him, and he took me away to the Cove of Cork. And that was the end of it.

ANEURIN. Except for the night before Camlann battle.

> You hoped, did you not
> To discover again that night
> The man who gave you such a fright
> Upon the marshland near your father's hall –
> And you were disappointed?

GWENDDYDD.

    Not at all.

ANEURIN.

    Yet you still do hope
    That he is still alive
    Or, being dead,
    He can be brought to life?
    You yet do think yourself
    To be mad Merlin's wife?
    It is not probable –
    It is not even desirable –
    Fifteen years have come and gone:
    Does he remember his old music?
    Does he remember the mud on your gown?

GWENDDYDD. I remember. Why not him?

ANEURIN.

    It is better not to meddle
    Even though you did laugh
    When he fell into his puddle.
    Girl, he is now in quite another puddle
    And he very well may drown.

GWENDDYDD.

    So pull him out.

ANEURIN.

    I have told you I will not.

Enter BEDWYR, *carrying a sheathed sword, with* COMPANIONS.

BEDWYR. Well?

GWENDDYDD. No.

BEDWYR. Not?

ANEURIN. Not.

BEDWYR. That's bad for you, boy. Indeed, from this decision, you must be a man of no good luck.

He draws the sword – it is ARTHUR'*s, with the point broken. (Not so much of it is broken that it cannot be used.) The* COMPANIONS *close in round* ANEURIN, *they have their swords out as well.*

ANEURIN. That sword has been brandished by a stronger hand than yours.

BEDWYR. Oh yes, it is the sword of Arthur. Of Magnus Maximus

the famous weapon. Enchanted, one might say, by the succession
of great warriors who have hooked it to their belt.

ANEURIN. And Arthur said to you when he left it with you – 'You
wear it for me: be my successor!' He said that?

BEDWYR. He did not. He did command me to throw it into deep
water. But God above, the man was dying – did he know what it
was he said? So haphazard an instruction – how can I obey it?
How can I? Tell me! Tell me how!

FIRST COMPANION. Don't ask us about that –

SECOND COMPANION. We have no authority in such matters.

BEDWYR. Exactly so. We *must* have Merlin! He will tell us what
should be done. So go, boy. Find him. Fetch him. I give you
orders – by this sword.

ANEURIN. Not sufficient.

BEDWYR. Then by these others which are not broken. You go. And
I keep *her*.

> *He suddenly grabs* GWENDDYDD *and tosses her in among the*
> COMPANIONS *who hold her tight. One of them lays his blade*
> *across her throat.*

I could kill her. I could marry her. Which would you like least?
One of them or the other will be done this minute before your
face . . . So make up your mind.

GWENDDYDD. Aneurin, my dearest love, for heaven's sake – will
you do what he wants you to do!

ANEURIN. But – one man running lunatic through the whole of the
Caledonian Forest – *I* don't know how to find him!

BEDWYR. You are a poet and he is a poet. You will know where he
will go. If you don't know, you will understand the right sort of
questions to ask. Until Merlin steps again across the bridge of
Carlisle fort, this woman of yours is kept behind bars and bolts
and very little she will get to eat. So bear it in mind.

> *Exeunt* BEDWYR *and* COMPANIONS *with* GWENDDYDD.

ANEURIN. You will tell me I should have protested. But sure they
would never treat her as badly as all that . . . ? After all, she wants
her Merlin quite as much as they do, so it seems. There is no
logic whatever upon either side of the question .(*He sings.*)
     The last command of Arthur was
     Haphazard as a wind-blown bird.

Bedwyr is like the wind himself –
Haphazard, haphazard is the only word –
I do not know where I should go
Haphazard is my only guide
I'll turn around around around –
Oh giddy, so giddy – where is my giddy road –?

As he sings he spins round and round, becomes dizzy, and lets himself fall down. Then he gets up again.

Which way was my head pointing? North? And a little east. Out of the cold north-east comes up the cruel winter. Don't like it, but I'll go there ...

SCENE FIVE

Woodland

ANEURIN *walks about the stage.*

ANEURIN (*singing*).
Haphazard and at random so
I pick my way with the wind in my eye.
Each man I meet I must inquire –
'Have you seen a naked madman fly ... ?'

The FARMER *enters on the last line of the song, carrying a spade.*

– by any chance ... ?

FARMER. I have seen madmen and dead men and men with their legs and arms cut off, and men in terror running miles and miles and miles across the moor – what else would you expect in the days after a great battle? (*He turns away rudely.*)

ANEURIN.
Got nothing out of him.
I'll take a quick drink from this stream
And then once more begin to trudge
Until I get to the world's black edge –

FARMER. Don't drink out of that, boy – the water is poisoned. There are the corpses of many soldiers who were all cut down at the ford.

ANEURIN. Arthur's men?

FARMER. How should I know whose? They held sharp weapons, did they not? And sharp weapons have held them! There is also a dead horse. If I could get them one by one above there into my small field, they would fertilize the ground for me, and appropriate too. I have a right to compensation. There were other frantic soldiers who ran away from the battle set fire to my house as they went; and all my beasts, and my wife, have been burnt. You will help me cut up the corpses, and give me a hand to bury them?

ANEURIN. By God, I will not.

FARMER. Then I will do it myself and be damned to you. On your way, boy, take your journey, or I will break open your head. (*He raises his spade menacingly.*)

ANEURIN *flees. Exit* FARMER. *Re-enter* ANEURIN.

ANEURIN. It would be better to inquire of all the madmen have they seen the one man who is *not* mad ... (*He sings.*)

At random and haphazard so
I pick my way with the rain upon my cheeks.
This old bent back once had no need
To stoop in the wild wood gathering sticks.

MORGAN *has entered, with a small bundle of twigs.*

Morgan – don't be frightened – I am a poet – I am your friend –

MORGAN. Don't see too good, old Morgan doesn't – no. Stand where you are – I have a knife – cut out your heart and liver as soon as touch you – yes, I could.

She recognizes him.

So: the men of the long sword have all laid down and died
And Morgan gathers wood to make a fire to cook her food.
Strathclyde is dead. He is dead as this dead wood.

ANEURIN. Yes.

MORGAN. He was the one that let me live, in the mill house at Carlisle, when all the rest would have killed me dead. He hated me, he was afraid of me, he let me have protection. Now I don't have any, so I ran off into the forest. A very proper place indeed to fall in with the ragged poet who gave his worship to none but to the splendid gay ladies – and what payment did he get? Come, put

your strong young arms around old Morgan – kiss her for the
memory!

ANEURIN *embraces her.*

ANEURIN.
      And here is the only memory, more or less,
      Of that tall and mischievous Princess
      Who gave her favours where she damn well chose
      To lords and gentlemen and braggarts of the land –
      They would kill each other for one touch of her white hand!
      According to her smile or to her wanton angry frown
      Great Princes were dragged down
      Wars were created, wars were prevented
      All sober Christian counsel was most ludicrously circum-
            vented.
      And now there is not one amorous nobleman
      To heap up her shoulders with fur and brocade of gold –
      Only a discredited poet
      Who never knew her at all
      Until she was old . . .
      There is another poet in this wood –
      Have you seen him, have you heard of him,
      Can you tell where his footsteps fall?
MORGAN. Merlin?
ANEURIN. Merlin.
MORGAN.
      Oh yes, he will run
      And he will cry
      And he will fly
      And he will call –
      Before ever he slept with a girl
      Or scraped the beard upon his chin
      He put his round black head into my lap
      And his fingers were spread out on my skin –
      'Madam, will you teach me, teach me, teach me . . . ?'
      Merlin's word to me, though you may not believe it,
      Merlin's word, and agreeably I did listen, I did receive it.
      Thirty-two good teeth I had,
      And he did count them, every one,
      Between his own teeth with his red tongue.

> What has happened to him since –
> Where has all his music gone?

ANEURIN. It's not his music I am looking for. I want *him*.

MORGAN. *You* do?

ANEURIN. His wife does.

MORGAN. Where is she?

ANEURIN. Carlisle.

MORGAN. She is a fool. Far too soon for him to be thinking of her. All he can think of now is what he can find to eat.

ANEURIN. What would he find, in winter, in this forest?

MORGAN. I found *this* . . . (*She pulls a dead rabbit out from among her rags.*)

ANEURIN. Who caught that for you – the ravens?

MORGAN. Or the red foxes.

ANEURIN. I have heard of vipers in the heather that would bring her eggs between their fangs. But would they do as much for Merlin? I think not.

MORGAN.

> The vipers and the squirrels and the badgers
> Curl up and sleep at this time of the year.
> Merlin does not sleep. He is led
> Through the treetops and through the air
> By a quiet crying in his left ear –
> The madman's voice that only madmen hear –

and it brings him to the beautiful glen that is hidden in the mountains of the north. They call it the Glen of the Madmen, because all of the madmen of Britain will go there, if they are let, by one and by two, they will go, to find restfulness and peace, and a cure for their frenzy –

ANEURIN. I have heard of this glen. I had no reason to think that it was more than a fable.

MORGAN. Most certainly no fable. The Glen is there. I have seen it myself. But it is no use your trying to go to it – Merlin will never leave that Glen until he has had enough of it, and that's not yet. The very shape of the place, you see, provides protection and nourishment for the madmen that will frequent it. It has four gaps to the wind and a thick sheltering wood, and wells it has, and springs, and sandy clearwater streams. And there in the streams is the watercress found. And there are sorrels and berries and wild garlic and black sloes and brown acorns – even in the heart of

winter there is something green to eat, for the madmen, when they
come. But not much – and to gain their portion of the watercress
they will strike each other bitterly, they will howl out loud in their
rage and in their greed for the curative herbs –

A clamour of MADMEN'*s voices is heard growing offstage.*
MORGAN *goes out.* ANEURIN *remains.*

A crowd of MADMEN (*and* WOMEN) *including* MERLIN *comes
running onto the stage. As soon as they are all onstage their
clamour suddenly stops; and they struggle furiously in silence over
the distribution of a bundle of watercress, which one of them holds
and is trying to keep for himself. Some of them get a share and
some do not. They all run off again, still disputing – as they leave
the stage their voices are raised again, and so fade away into the
distance.* MERLIN *remains behind. He has one handful of cress.*

*His costume is his Mad Outfit. It consists of a mask – a moderately
distorted copy of the actor's face, with beard grown and hair quite
long – and an overall fleshing of skin-colour streaked with green
and red and covered with black hair in patches. If anything is left
of his breechclout it is now no more than fringe of ripped and filthy
rags.*

He is nervous after the fight with the other MADMEN, *and he
cautiously begins to climb up a post at the side of the stage.*

ANEURIN (*on forestage*).
  Now they howl out loud and then
  Dead silence in the lonely Glen.
  That is the only way the mad folk find
  To tell each other what is in their mind –
  To tell each other, and to tell themselves:
  Yet they are men and women and not wolves.
  God gave a talking tongue to Baalam's Ass.
  For crazy Merlin I can do no less –
  This is what he would be saying now
  If only he could remember how –

  Speaking for MERLIN.

  A handful of watercress
  It is not much to hold.
  My fingers are so cold –
  I think I must have dropped some –

My one handful of watercress
And now I have so much less.
I do not know how long it has been
I have crouched in the dark branches of the tree.
The ebbtide has gone out
The floodtide has not come in
Neither water nor earth nor fire is huddled around me
The only blanket for my wounded skin
Is the shifting sliding crawling invisible cold wind
That moves over me for longer
Than the long march of a great army –
But an army without commanders,
Without music, without brave banners
No rest at night in its encampment
No women nor hot meat for its bodily enjoyment
No wine for its thirsty soldiers to drink
No hope for a rich victory
No celebration of success in the metres of accomplished
    poetry –
Oh why and when did Merlin ever dream
That men of power and progress and authoritative domain
Would keep his pale blood warmer
Than a little green plant that grows in the running stream . . . ?

MERLIN *drops his watercress, and falls down in the effort to re-
trieve it.*

MERLIN. Dropped it – I must find it –!
ANEURIN (*speaking for* MERLIN).
    It's getting dark – it will be stolen away –
    These madmen are such thieves, you see,
    Their eyesight in the night is twice as sharp as in the day –
    Oh God, how can I get back again . . . ?

MERLIN *struggles to climb up to his perch once more, but he keeps
slipping and falling. At last he does it.*

Who could believe that a naked man
Would fight and fight until he won
His furious battle all alone
Against the sword-blades of the naked thorn?

MERLIN *and* ANEURIN (*together*).

>Here is my tree and I have conquered it
>It draws blood where I clutch it and blood where I sit.
>I used to stand aside and watch the battles from afar –
>Now I take part in them, I am both trooper and great general,
>Proud wielder of Imperium, sole director of the war!

Lights go out except for one on MERLIN's *face.*
Exit ANEURIN. *Then, all lights out.*
MERLIN *climbs down and goes out, in the darkness.*

SCENE SIX

Mill.

Enter FIRST COMPANION *leading* GWENDDYDD *by a rope tied around her waist. She is in a bad way, neglected and unkempt.*
The MILLER *comes back and forwards across the stage, carrying sacks of flour, etc.*

FIRST COMPANION (*tugging viciously on the rope*). Goddammit, girl, you are damned fortunate, to be held here in this mill – yes, in some comfort – oh, you could be inside the fort, there is a black hole inside the fort – you could well be locked up in that – such great consideration has been shown you, and with neither word nor look d'you indicate yourself aware of it! Five Red Wounds of Jesus; but how I hate a woman so neglectful of herself and of all that's done for her! She will neither wash herself nor eat nor put a comb into her hair. She will not even talk to herself, let alone to anyone else. Did I ask as a special favour to be put here to watch over her?

MILLER. Did you what? I can't hear you. Moreover you are obstructing me in the operation of my mill.

FIRST COMPANION. The one of them is dumb and the other is as deaf as his own granite grinding-stones. For such bloody nonsense as this, is it, we survived the slaughter of Camlann! I have in mind to get a bucket of cold water and thoroughly scrub the stinking bitch.

MILLER. You don't do violence here.

FIRST COMPANION. So you can hear what I say, then?

MILLER. I am aware of you, you broken soldier, I am aware you utter threats. It is your trade, when all is said. My trade is to grind up corn, I have my wheels here with their great teeth: they are the good tools of my trade. When you are dead and all your sons are dead, this craftwork will be needed, by the heathen English or whoever else. And so, it is protected, and those within my walls remain protected too. Why don't you leave us? She won't escape. Why ever should she? When she waits here every day for her poet to come back to her.

GWENDDYDD. Which poet? *Which!*

MILLER. You tell me then, I don't know.

GWENDDYDD. Neither do I, God help me, that's where the trouble is.

MILLER. I don't hear you . . . Go on, go on, why don't you go?

The COMPANION *glares, irresolute.*

He has no orders from his Captain, that's why not . . .

FIRST COMPANION. And that's enough of *that!*

MILLER. You know who I saw today? Old Morgan. In the wood, hunting about and muttering – it was either her or a rat from the river-bank. She will be back here, broken soldier, and then what will you do?

FIRST COMPANION (*crossing himself*). Morgan –?

MILLER. She will turn you into a hedgehog. Indeed yes, she has that power.

FIRST COMPANION. Ah to the devil. Can't abide it. Go and throw some dice with my Companions in the fort . . . (*Exits.*)

MILLER. Hey, but wait, you have no orders – sent him off as fast as a cut cat, that did – ho, ho, they're all afraid of *her*. Why else did they let her live here all these years? Didn't worry *me* she stayed here – you may have noticed I'm a little deaf, my dear, could never catch her nasty language – hurt me nothing.

GWENDDYDD. If she does come back, will they kill her?

MILLER. What's that? . . . Oh . . . Oh no – for what could I not put in the grain that I grind for their dinners? (*Exit.*)

GWENDDYDD *sits down hopelessly in the corner. Enter* BEDWYR *and* FIRST COMPANION *on forestage.*

FIRST COMPANION. Can't abide it. Keep your own guard. God damn the dirty strumpet, she's not going to get away.

BEDWYR. I gave you orders – you have broken them.

FIRST COMPANION. There are very few men, Captain, to whom you can give orders at all, at this present time. I wonder you do not select your instructions with more regard for their importance.

BEDWYR (*after a pause*). So that's the way of it . . . Indeed yes, this matter is but trivial. You may go.

> *Exit* FIRST COMPANION. BEDWYR *calls after him.*

But you hold yourself in readiness for any further commands I may give you! (*Exit.*)

> *Enter* MORGAN, *very slowly and cautiously, looking behind all the wings of the stage in case she is observed. When she feels herself safe enough she comes and sits down beside* GWENDDYDD *and puts her arms around her.*

MORGAN. I'm back, you see. You knew I would be here? Oh, *I* saw the soldier go . . .

> MORGAN *takes hold of* GWENDDYDD's *rope and wraps it around her own waist, and then the two of them go out, linked together.*

SCENE SEVEN

Snowscape.

Enter ANEURIN.

ANEURIN (*singing*).
> Outside the bounds of the Madmen's Glen
> I made my camp and there did lie.
> Sooner or later he must come out
> And I will catch him as he hurtles by.
> It is Christmas Day – five hundred years
> Since God was born in Bethlehem
> But there in the snow at the edge of the Glen
> Is the dark foot-print of Herod King.

MERLIN *appears at the top of one of the stageposts. He wears his Mad Outfit.*

ANEURIN (*looking first at the footprints and then at his own shoes*). And these are the shoes that made it. Will it frighten him away when he comes out? If it does, he is not ready for me. It if does not, then I am ready for him – and may God help him when he discovers to what it is he has been led. (*He rolls himself up in his cloak and sleeps on the forestage.*)

MERLIN.
Cold is the snow
All green has gone
To black-and-white;

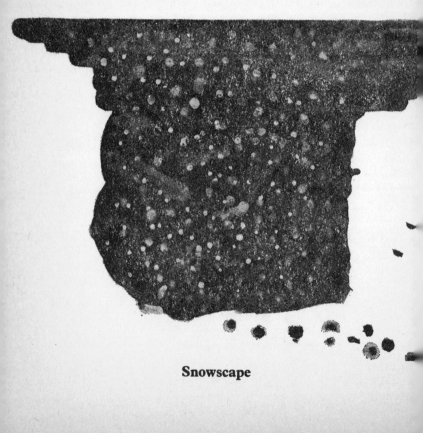

Snowscape

My Kingdom come –
I do not know
How to hold it
Where to go.
My hands are shaking and my side,
There is confusion far and wide
Between the wan waters of Forth and Clyde.
All Caledonia waves and swoops in fear –
Go there, go there
Come here, come here –
I will not go, I cannot come
I have but a wooden horse to ride upon
And he is rooted in the ground.
Against the thunder of the roaring wind
Black feathers are the armour for my skin.
The ramparts and the bastions that surround
My stronghold at the top end of this Glen
Are built of ivy-bush and holly – they were green
But in this white of winter raven-black they seem –
Dark as the oak-tree is my beaten head
And dark my lacerated loin –
Oh God, where is Your godlike beard of green . . . ?

MERLIN *sees the footprints and scrambles down to examine them more closely.*

Man
And not mad
For he has walked out of the Glen.

Very carefully he follows the tracks, now and then bolting back into cover at the suspicion of a noise. He smells at the tracks like a dog. Then he sees ANEURIN. *He withdraws, and watches him from a distance.*

There he lies, under the wall.
He is asleep, I can hear him snore.
To sleep like that I do not dare.
Not to sleep – in time of war!
The teeth of wolves would travel at me, tear me open.
I close my eyes at night, quite often.
But then immediately my heart will quake

And I will wake
And so remember, to my pain,
That though today is Monday
Tomorrow will not be Tuesday –
No, nor never again . . .

*He runs off, and then slowly comes back. This time he turns to the
audience and addresses them directly.*

Now listen to me, young gentlemen, you aspire to be poets? If
you did not, your fathers would not have sent you to me to be my
pupils, so I assume that you all do. You aspire to be poets and
yet you show not the slightest grasp of the rudiments of the
observance of nature. Without which no true poet can ever – and
so on and so forth – as you have heard from me *ad nauseam!*
So here is a little test for you. The sun has gone down. First proof
of the observation? It is dark, and the moon is up. Second proof?
There is a fellow here asleep. People do not sleep in the afternoon,
in open air, in winter. Unless they are mad. We have already
determined that he cannot be that. Now then, from your large
experience, from your abundant observation of the working of
cause and effect – what will happen next? Come on, come on,
come on – pray make use of your tiny minds – yes, you sir, at the
back there, you have an answer, what is it? . . . Not bad, not bad at
all . . . now put it into verse as you have been taught and let all the
class receive the benefit of your muse!
The sun will rise
The man will awake
He will stand on his feet
And give himself a shake!
Good, boy, very good! . . . I wonder if he will. If he doesn't, it
will prove that everything I have been telling them for all these
years was quite wrong from the very beginning . . .

ANEURIN *wakes up.*

But oh no, it was not wrong. I have remembered it quite cor-
rectly. Though maybe did I use to tell them rather more than I
have remembered . . . ? But this, for a start, is not bad. He is a
man, and he wakes up . . . But just a moment, he is more than
that. He is a man: and a poet. And that cannot be correct.
Because of all the poetry I made an end –

I did it with a spear in my right hand.
He has come here to make an end of me.
Poet, keep out of the sight of the poet:
Do not, do not, do not let him see . . .

He climbs up the post again.

ANEURIN. Breaking of twigs I heard. He has been moving in the treetops. He will have seen me while I was asleep. How the devil am I ever going to see *him*, though? That's the question. If I look for the broken twigs, on the ground here, under the branches, it stands to reason I must come at last to the tree where he is hid.

MERLIN. So he looks for me – he follows me – I won't let him do that. It is I that will follow *him*. Crafty, it will be – guileful – I shall deceive him altogether . . .

ANEURIN. If he will not be found, then never will I be able to find him. Not haphazard, not at random: logic. So what to do?

The next point of the logic
Without doubt appears to be
That if *I* can't follow *him*
Perhaps *he* will follow *me* . . .

But for what reason? Food? I have no food. His wife? No . . . Poetry? Perhaps. But what sort? His own sort? Not any more. My sort? I don't suppose so. He's neither a tinker nor a bandit, though he does live in the wild wood. I wonder should I not go back then, far back beyond the fen country and the wet mud on Gwenddydd's haunches, far back beyond the foolish day when he counted Morgan's teeth for her . . . What about this?

He takes a little drum that hangs at his belt – or perhaps a tambourine – and starts beating out a nursery rhythm, humming and whistling the tune before he begins on the words of the song. He sings.

I was born a piper's son
I played my pipe when I was young
And all the tunes that I could play
Was over the hills and far away.
Over the hills and a great way off
The wind has blown my topknot off.

MERLIN *has begun to stir and to come nearer.* ANEURIN *walks about the stage as he sings. He is careful not to turn and catch*

MERLIN's *eye*. MERLIN *starts to follow him – at first some way off, and then closer.*

I never knew what I had done
That every time I came to town
The people first would dance and play
And then would chase me clean away.
Over the hills and a great way off
The wind has blown my topknot off.

MERLIN *is now dancing behind* ANEURIN.

So bright and free their hearts would range
You would not think they'd ever change –
But teeth came out and eyes went in
And still I played the self-same tune.
Over the hills and a great way off
The wind has blown my topknot off.

ANEURIN *goes out, still singing.* MERLIN *prances after him, just as he goes he bursts into song himself – singing the refrain 'Over the hills and a great way off,' etc.*
Enter BEDWYR.

BEDWYR. Word comes from the north-east coast, as I knew that it would, but not so soon. The heathen have brought over all their people out of Germany. So terrible was their voyage too, huge waves, storms of sleet, ice – one third of their keels turned over and foundered, but none the less they came. I cannot but wonder at the crude courage of them, how desperate they must have been. Women they have brought with them, children, cattle and sheep and goats and pigs. They have extended themselves all over the boundaries of Gododdin, they have cut down trees and built houses, they have had the nerve to lay out farms upon the bleakest parts of the moor. Moreover, they have erected certain lumps of unsmoothed wood to represent their barbarous gods. In front of which, their fires of sacrifice . . . Oh God, when will they come to take Carlisle? I cannot keep them out. The new Prince of Strathclyde is a child of five years old, the Prince of Gododdin has locked himself into his fortress in fear, and the great Army of the Red Dragon is what you have seen it to be. Where is Merlin, where is Merlin – where!

ANEURIN *is heard singing offstage. He comes in at the back with* MERLIN, *as before, capering behind.* (MERLIN *is still in the same costume.*) MERLIN *joins in the refrains of each verse.*

ANEURIN (*singing*).
> I did not know, I could not learn
> What fury in their hearts would burn
> Or why they ran with murder dark
> To cut my throat and eat my heart.
> Over the hills and a great way off
> The wind has blown my topknot off.

> When I escaped I always swore
> That I would play my pipe no more.
> Yet there I would be the very next day
> With over the hills and far away.
> Over the hills and a great way off
> The wind has blown my topknot off.

As he sings the above stanzas he has led MERLIN *in and out of the wings and across the stage in a zigzag pattern, and during the last stanza he leads him out altogether. His voice is heard offstage. When he comes to the end of the words, he and* MERLIN *are heard humming and whistling the tune and the beat of their feet is heard throughout the ensuing dialogue, also the beat of* ANEURIN's *drum.*

BEDWYR (*clapping his hands*). Companions – to me – here – quickly!

Enter COMPANIONS.

Merlin comes home! He must be taken at the river-crossing – and taken quickly with no mischance. Bring him straight into the fort . . . Don't just stand there and look at me – do it! It is quick work and not difficult – it will be finished in a few moments!

SECOND COMPANION. We will need a coil of rope.

FIRST COMPANION. I will obtain one.

He goes out and returns at once with rope.

BEDWYR. Good. And there is one thing more – that nasty wife of his who lies so stubborn in the millhouse, must be given no word of what has been done. Very well: here is the river – and here are the two travellers – we let the first one cross . . .

Two of the COMPANIONS *pick up a long blue strip of cloth that is ready at the side of the forestage. They stretch this out across the stage to represent the river.* BEDWYR *and the other* COMPANIONS *lie in wait.* ANEURIN, *still playing his drum, comes in and passes across behind the blue cloth. When he gets to the far end of it* BEDWYR *seizes him from behind, puts his hand over his mouth and a dagger into his back, and holds him still in the corner.* MERLIN *enters, dancing and making music with his mouth and two sticks which he claps together.*

MERLIN (*singing as he crosses the river*).
Over the hills and a great way off.
The wind has blown my topknot off . . .

BEDWYR *gives a signal. The* COMPANIONS *fall upon* MERLIN *in the middle of the river. There is a struggle, the blue cloth is violently agitated, hiding the men from sight.* MERLIN, *underneath it, screams. Then it is suddenly withdrawn. The* COMPANIONS *have* MERLIN *and are rapidly winding ropes around his body – leaving his legs free and also two ends of the rope to pull him along with.*

BEDWYR (*to* ANEURIN, *as he takes his hand away from his mouth*).
Do not say what you are about to say. You have done what I told you, and that is enough. There is a man of medicine in Carlisle, a scholar on his way to Ireland lately shipwrecked upon this coast – I swear to you in the name of the dragon-banner I once carried that I will send for him to Merlin's bedside and let him work what cure he can.

The COMPANIONS, *having secured* MERLIN *and removed the blue cloth now bring him round the stage and down in a kind of mock triumph.* MERLIN *walks in a daze – apparently quite unaware of what is being done to him.*

COMPANIONS (*in a barbarous chant*).
Bedwyr Bedwyr
Your Poet is here
Ask him what you want to know
And he will answer yes or no!

They give a cheer and lead him out.

SCENE EIGHT

Fort.

ANEURIN *is about to leave.*

BEDWYR. You will *not* go to the mill.

> ANEURIN *obeys him and goes out on the other side from the one*
> *he had originally intended.*
> *Enter* TALIESIN, *still swathed in bandages, and hobbling with the*
> *aid of his staff. With him is the* DOCTOR.

TALIESIN. It is not possible – he cannot have come back!

DOCTOR. Now look here, sir, I have told you that any endeavour at
locomotion in the present state of your recovery is exceedingly
deleterious. You really must resume your bed –

TALIESIN. Captain – you are acting in contravention of my curse!
Moreover, I have been told that you intend to take this doctor
from me and have him minister to Merlin. Is this true?

BEDWYR. Not true. He ministers to both of you. Why, man, you
don't require him every hour of every day. You are already upon
the mend.

DOCTOR. Exactly so, upon the mend. For observe, I have put hot
fomentations of pigeons' dung against his feet, an appropriate
tree-fungus soaked in squirrel's urine thrust under his arm-
pits and groin, and of course the traditional periodic application
of leeches – though your Cumbrian leech is a very poor sort of
creature indeed. I estimate a matter of seventeen weeks only,
before he is fit to walk. D'ye hear that, sir – so back to bed with
you! His wound is still inflamed. To be sure, it was deep enough,
and I think the spear was dirty. If he'd only obey my orders I
could go home to Ireland at once and leave him with a quiet mind.

BEDWYR. You don't go home yet.

DOCTOR. Indeed there is no ship.

BEDWYR. No sir, nor will there be until Merlin has been cured.

DOCTOR. Captain, that's no way to talk to a conscientious practi-
tioner!

BEDWYR. If you were conscientious you would stay with your

patients! For what good will you do in Ireland? They know nothing of you there.

DOCTOR. Which is exactly why I want to be there. Ah sure, they have the Gospel now among the rocks of Connemara, but of the rudiments of humane science they are, alas, entirely ignorant. Why else have I lived in Egypt for the last five years but to fill myself with the study of the wise men of Greece and Rome and then return in my prime to benefit my poor countrymen. It is an act of small nobility to balk me in such a work.

TALIESIN. It is an act of no nobility at all to balk me in my sacred commination!

BEDWYR. On the day of my General's death you showed yourself disloyal to all that he stood for. I have nothing to say to you.

TALIESIN. Merlin is my victim. I will not have him saved!

DOCTOR. I have told you you must not excite yourself!

TALIESIN. Physician, in his physic, I exhort you to put ratsbane!

DOCTOR. A most incorrect sentiment.

TALIESIN *falls.*

Come along now, I gave you warning – is it dead within the week you want to be? (*To* BEDWYR.) But you have promised to find a ship for me – you'll not forget that?

BEDWYR. *If* you can cure Merlin.

DOCTOR. If, indeed – of course I'll cure him! (*He helps* TALIESIN *out.*)

BEDWYR. Let both of them protest for as long as they will – I have constituted myself Captain of this fort of Carlisle, and my orders are to be obeyed.

Enter COMPANIONS.

FIRST COMPANION. The question is, for how long? I mean, what do we do now? We have him safe strapped down to a plank in a little room with no windows. But what about it? I mean – what's the purpose –?

SECOND COMPANION. I mean, as far as I can see, we might just as well disperse ourselves about the country, turn bandit, what's wrong with that?

THIRD COMPANION. Merlin or no Merlin, we cannot defend Carlisle.

BEDWYR. Companions: for the sake of the memory of Arthur, I beg you keep together until this business is resolved. I swear to you in the name of the dragon-banner I once carried that if we find that there is nothing further that can be done, then nothing further shall be done. But the sword of Maximus Emperor is still waiting for a hand to clutch it, and I must find out for certain whether that hand is mine. If it is, you are my men, and you will obey me, that I know. If not, then a band of robbers is all that you are fit for – though in my opinion you are too old for it.

FIRST COMPANION. And if not, then what will you do – will you fight the heathen by yourself?

BEDWYR. Old soldier, I will do just that. Not with a sword. But I will do it. (*Exit*.)

FIRST COMPANION. I think he's gone mad.

SECOND COMPANION. I think Arthur went mad.

THIRD COMPANION. We know that Merlin *is*.

FIRST COMPANION. I think we'd better wait and see.

Exeunt.

SCENE NINE

Mill.

Enter ANEURIN.

ANEURIN (*singing*).
You will not go to the mill, he said.
He did not say why, so I went to the mill.
Outside was a man with a sword in his hand
And the door was barred with a bolt of steel.

THIRD COMPANION *enters, with drawn sword, behind* ANEURIN.

THIRD COMPANION. Caught you! It's no good, boy. You turn around and go, or I put this through you. No question – I will do it.

ANEURIN. Who have you got in there? His wife, is it?

THIRD COMPANION. No good, boy –

ANEURIN (*calling loudly*). Gwenddydd!

THIRD COMPANION. I said – go –

He makes a run at ANEURIN, *who dodges and scurries off. He does not leave altogether, though – he gets down on to the forestage and crouches there.*

MORGAN'S VOICE (*singing behind backcloth*).
    One morning I walked out and I walked upon the green
    It was there that I met with a young man so curious to be seen –
THIRD COMPANION. You hold your noise in there – you black hag
    –hold it! I'll come in on you and carve your windpipe –!
ANEURIN. But he won't – he is shaking terrified.
MORGAN'S VOICE (*singing behind backcloth*).
    For he wandered not upon his feet but upon the palm of his
        hands
    The world is upside-down
    Oh who has turned it?
    I saw this little bold fellow and I tell you no lie
    In a four-cornered enclosure they had him roped and tied
    Where before like a wild roebuck he would rove both far and
        wide
    The world was upside-down
    And he was laughing.
THIRD COMPANION (*calling*). What was that then? Who told *you*
    of it? *I* didn't – I was ordered not to, so they can't put the blame
    upon *me* –
ANEURIN. But roped and tied he is, and she is aware of it, somehow.
    And now Gwenddydd is aware of it, because I know she is inside
    there too – and what in God's name is Gwenddydd going to do?

    GWENDDYDD, *behind backcloth, moans and sobs.*

Gwenddydd is going to do nothing because there is nothing she
can do. Her own fault, she would have him, but she would not
have him compelled. Not possible at all – the one without the
other. I'm having no more to do with this!

    He gets up and goes over to the COMPANION.

I'm having nothing more to do with it.
THIRD COMPANION. That's right, boy, that's bloody sensible.
ANEURIN.
    Yet Gwenddydd is a fair young woman
    I have known her well for many a year

And the sound of her grief in the dark millhouse
Is twice as much as I can bear . . .

Enter BEDWYR.

BEDWYR. You were about to go away.

ANEURIN. I was. But I hesitated.

BEDWYR. Good that you did hesitate. I have more work for you yet. That Doctor is quite useless.

ANEURIN. Oh yes, he would be.

BEDWYR. But you, you made music in the forest, and Merlin followed the music. At this moment he follows nothing. He is stretched out upon his plank of wood, he stares up into the dark but only with the whites of his eyes – the pupils of them are turned downwards, inwards, glaring into his own brain. What is it that he can see there . . . ? Play music, more music – sing to him, why can't you? *Bring him back to life!*

ANEURIN. You forget, when I did make music, that music was interrupted. No damned good to begin it again.

BEDWYR. So what do you suggest?

ANEURIN. You are *asking* my advice?

BEDWYR. Your *opinion,* if nothing else. Though it is driving a screw of brass into the back of my neck to have to do it.

ANEURIN. Very well then:
    I suggest to you that from this day
    You handle poor mad Merlin never again.
    He will not be of use to you again.
    He will not be of use to any man.
    He has been used by far too many far too long.
    He desired to be a poet: he desired to make a song.
    He desired to make it for himself alone
    And for a girl, could he find one to love.
    And that is all a poet needs to move
    His heart to set his brain to match his words together.

BEDWYR.
    But you did march your own words in quite a different order
    When you made use of them to pile that slut
    Gwenhwyvar into the bed of Medraut –
    I need not tell you what you brought about –
    You can't deny it, poet, you did make use.
    Or you were made use of – you take your choice –

ANEURIN.

> Against my will they did destroy my voice.
> So I tell you, it must not be done again
> What has been done already –
> From experience I tell you
> For I know how it is done –
> Merlin is his own man
> He is to be handled by nobody.
> You could let him be with his wife . . .

BEDWYR.

> No. For she led an irregular life.
> Salacious, was she not? Gwenhwyvar's companion.

ANEURIN.

> You could let him be with Morgan.
> When he was a young man, it is said she was his love.

BEDWYR.

> Morgan is a condemned devil.
> She is observed by God above:
> She is observed, she will be sent
> In God's good time to endless punishment.
> And so will you. I have no more to say.
> You will go out of Carlisle this very day.

He claps his hand and calls.

Companions!

The COMPANIONS *enter.*

> Drive him out.
> With great brutality humiliate him,
> Kick him and beat him and send him upon his way.

The COMPANIONS *obey.*

So where is the Doctor!

COMPANIONS. Doctor!

Enter the DOCTOR.

BEDWYR. Well?

DOCTOR. Do you know, I have come to the conclusion that the problem is beyond my capacity. To begin with, I had some sort of notion that we might try what you'd call the 'Sympathetic Treatment'.

BEDWYR. Well?

DOCTOR. Your man Merlin is under a curse from Taliesin, is he not? Taliesin refuses to lift off the curse. Unless he is *compelled*, which wouldn't be very politic. Begod, he would put a curse upon ourselves if we tried that. But if we could convey from Taliesin, a portion of his bodily humours – beneficent humours, it goes without saying – and insert the said humours into the physiology of Merlin, then perhaps the trick could be worked, and Taliesin the whole while kept in complete ignorance. Good. So I took an eviscerated toad – always a very useful Agent of Transference – with the aim of applying it to Taliesin's chest for twelve hours and then placing it upon Merlin . . . It could be done – it *has* been done – I can't find any fault with the theory. But Lord save us, Taliesin would have nothing to do with the toad. Indeed, he threw it in my face.

BEDWYR. You were astonished?

DOCTOR. I was outraged! Permit me to assist you, Captain, to a better understanding of the internal influences of the common-or-garden toad. Now the toad –

BEDWYR. I don't give a damn for the internal influences of the toad.

The COMPANIONS *are all laughing.*
BEDWYR *turns on them.*

Be quiet!

THIRD COMPANION. Ah to hell with it – we've done enough!

DOCTOR. A word with you in private, Captain – as it were, withdraw our hems from the contagion of this ribaldry . . .

He leads BEDWYR *away from the* COMPANIONS.

BEDWYR. Well?

DOCTOR. There is no question: Taliesin is absolutely adamant. But can we not forage a little and find out someone else who could lift this curse off Merlin? I mean – some class of an exorcist?

BEDWYR. You mean a priest?

DOCTOR. A priest perhaps . . .

BEDWYR. Now look you: I've told this to nobody. If I pass it on to you it is in the most occult secrecy.

DOCTOR. I'm a professional medical man, so . . .

BEDWYR. So . . . Arthur my General had heavier deeds upon his conscience than any other Christian I have ever met. Yet on the night before his death he refused to speak to a priest.

DOCTOR. Oh dear God, Captain, what a horrible thing.

BEDWYR. Consider this: he drove the clergymen from him with threats and with blows of his gauntlet. Is it likely any one of them will intervene to save his poet? His poet who was so loyal to him?

MERLIN. Did not Merlin in his work uphold the truth of Christianity?

BEDWYR. But Taliesin did as well. And by the account of the Church he was the more orthodox of the pair.

DOCTOR. Yes, a priest would be no good . . . A sorcerer . . . Black witchcraft . . .

BEDWYR. You said *what*?

DOCTOR. I said nothing . . . I suggest nothing . . . I just drop off a small notion, if you are acute enough to catch my drift . . . as a man of science, you understand, I will have no sort of involvement in anything of the kind . . . Captain, there is a cranky old sailing-boat moored at the mouth of the River Eden. The skipper is almost agreeable to attempt a voyage to the Irish coast. But he just does need one word from you . . . (Exit.)

BEDWYR (*to the* COMPANIONS). You are all accoutred in the soldier's noble gear, yet your posture is that of degraded beggars at the foul entry of a marketplace.

FIRST COMPANION. Very probable. We've done enough.

BEDWYR. No no, by God – not yet! One more chance. Take Gwenddydd out of the mill. Put her into the fort. Take Merlin out of the fort, put him into the mill. Do not let them see each other.

FIRST COMPANION. And Morgan?

BEDWYR. You will let Morgan alone. Most strictly alone. Set about it. *Fac hoc!*

FIRST COMPANION (*after a pause*). *Iussa tua comprehendimus et perficiemus.*

> *Exeunt all save* BEDWYR.
> *One of the* COMPANIONS *pulls* GWENDDYDD *across the stage and out. Two of them bring in* MERLIN, *strapped to a plank, and set him down in the middle of the stage. He is still wearing his Mad Outfit. But a loose dirty shirt has been put on him.*

MORGAN *comes in, looks carefully round, fails to see* BEDWYR —
who is pressed against the corner — and sits down beside MERLIN.
She unfastens his bonds.
BEDWYR *slips quietly out.*
MORGAN *begins to croon over* MERLIN *and then tickles him
violently. He sits up like a man just awakened from a normal sleep
– giggling.*

MERLIN. Oh, for Godsake give over – I can't bear to be tickled –
MORGAN. Come on, boy, you terrible lazybones, bright morning it
  is – sunshine – high time to get up!
MERLIN. Oh stop it, don't you hear me – I am getting out of bed . . .
  What has happened to my clothes –? No, wait a moment – where
  am I? I am not in my bed . . . This is the mill, at Carlisle! And
  you are old Morgan, who lives in the mill. You had better be
  careful, old lady – your brother the General believes that you are
  dead. If he discovers you are still here – on the fringes of his
  Army –
MORGAN. Oho – yes. Terrible time for old Morgan that will be –
  won't it?
MERLIN. But how did I get in here?
MORGAN. You were drunk.
MERLIN. When was I drunk? Where?
MORGAN. Last night at the dinner table of Chief Dragon, in his hall,
  you were drunk.
MERLIN. In his hall at Carlisle?
MORGAN. You were singing your songs to the General when he had
  eaten, but the strong wine came so over you, you were unable to
  finish – vomit across the table and all down your good blue robe.
  Oh, disgusted was Chief Dragon. He had his orderlies carry you
  out, then on your own feet away in the dark you staggered – and
  at the end you fetched up here.
MERLIN. Oh dear heaven, this is not credible! Oh, what have I done
  to my dignity and my status?
MORGAN. And what have you done to old Morgan in the night,
  forcing yourself on top of her, bare as a chicken's wish-bone?
MERLIN. No – no – I cannot – I can *not* have done that –!
MORGAN. Oh, you did – I was too old for it, but I did my best to
  make you happy. You used such words to me – I was your duck, I

was your rainbow – I was your little love who smelt of honeysuckle. It was not any honeysuckle that you were smelling of, my dear, but I was kind enough, and I endured it.

MERLIN. No, no, no –

He suddenly begins to roar with laughter.

– you mad old hag, with any man in any state you would do it, and God but in the morning you would laugh at him and kiss him –

They both laugh like crazy and hug each other.

– Lord, what will he say to me? He will deprive me of my office?

MORGAN. Like as not.

MERLIN (*laughing again*). And who the hell cares if he does? What am I? A Chief Poet? I ornament with polished euphony the coarse words of the General's thought. And the General's thought is always of dead men – you can't ornament *those*.

MORGAN. Sweet and decorous, they tell me, to lie down dead in battle on behalf of your native land.

MERLIN. Perhaps – if you are a soldier. But a Chief Poet is not a soldier. It is not *me* that will lie down dead. Why don't I keep quiet about it then? It looks like I have lost my robe . . .

MORGAN. Covered with horrid sick, and you threw it into a ditch.

MERLIN. I am not going to pull it out again. I shall remain naked. I shall rejoice in it. I don't rejoice in *this* –

He pulls off the coarse shirt he is wearing and throws it away.

I shall look for a young girl – two of them – three – and astonish them by my virility.

MORGAN. And what about old Morgan?

MERLIN. Oh, you as well, if you want to
    We shall inhabit the green forest
    And live alone in it forever.
    The sun will keep us warm
    We shall swim in the golden river
    We shall build our little house
    Out of brambles and bunches of fern
    And stretched out upon a bed of heather
    I will love each one of you in turn.

MORGAN. And your poetry?

MERLIN.

    All day long I will make it.

    Not only with music and words

    But with every muscle and every nerve –

    Touch and taste and hearing and sight and smell –

    Never before, will they say,

    Has Merlin done his work so well!

Oh – how I am hungry. Is there anything to eat?

MORGAN. Something light on your stomach, I think, to begin with. You voided it up with such violence last night. Best to be careful and let the digestion recover.

MERLIN. Watercress?

MORGAN. The very thing. It grows at the edge of the millpond. I will fetch you one handful.

    She leaves him, walks round, and comes downstage.
    BEDWYR *comes out from the wings catches her as he had previously caught* ANEURIN, *and holds her fast.*

BEDWYR. I was sitting outside the mill with my ear to the plank of the wall. Heard every word you said. Now then, I let you go. You will conduct yourself discreetly?

    She nods. He lets go and stands away; but still keeps his dagger out.

So: he knows who he is and where he is. But he does not know *when* he is, or what has happened for – how long? Six months, maybe longer? Now then: who's to tell him?

MORGAN. There is nothing more to be told to him until the broken sword is thrown away.

BEDWYR. Morgan, I am not afraid of you. I am a protected Christian, loyal to my Lord God. I will build a fire of sticks and put you on it and burn you to death. Look at me in the face. Do I mean what I say?

MORGAN. Cruel, cruel, you old man. You would torture an old woman to death.

BEDWYR. So you don't talk to me about that sword. Merlin must talk about the sword. Merlin and no one else.

MORGAN. You are not afraid of Morgan. Morgan is afraid of you. What do you want me to do?

BEDWYR. Take into him his watercress. Stay with him in the mill, Turn him once more into a Chief Poet who is not mad.

> *She nods and goes away, back to* MERLIN. BEDWYR *withdraws again into the wings.* MERLIN *is feeling his hair and his beard doubtfully.*

MERLIN. It's cold.

MORGAN (*giving him the cress*). Oh no, not so cold.

MERLIN. Did I not, when I was Chief Poet, use to cut my hair and shave my face?

MORGAN. Not as often as you thought you did.

MERLIN. I have a recollection . . . that lately . . . for some reason . . . I have done a great deal of running and jumping and scrambling about.

MORGAN. You were working so hard at the perfection of your art.

MERLIN. But all to no purpose – yes?

MORGAN. Yes. Why don't you eat your watercress?

MERLIN (*eating it*). Ah, it is good . . . after all that hard work, very good to eat watercress . . .

> It is good after long leaping
> To sit quiet on the floor –
> It is good after rain and hailstorm
> To keep tight shut the door.

MORGAN.

> It is good after long leaping
> To remember how far you flew.
> Not a stag on the highest mountain
> Ever sprang so fast as you.

MERLIN.

> From treetop to treetop
> My path was fierce and hard
> It cost me such grief
> But in the end I endured.

MORGAN.

> You endured it and you conquered
> You were the wildest wolf of all
> You are worthy on your welcome home
> To be greeted with cry and call
> 'Here is a King who went forth on the hill
> Alone and unarmed, his proud enemy to kill

And now he has returned again, all his prisoners behind,
Wolves and foxes, stags and eagles, every creature in his kind.
Their teeth are held close and their claws are drawn in,
Loyal servants are they all to our grave and stately King.'
Is that what you heard them shout when you last entered Carlisle?

MERLIN. Is it? . . . I did hear shouting – yes . . . but the words were
not the same . . .

*He picks up the ropes that had bound him to his plank and looks at
them, puzzled.*

I went out against a proud enemy? Did I? Who was it –?
Whom did I kill?

BEDWYR *and the* DOCTOR *have crept in to listen.*

DOCTOR (*in a sudden very loud shout*). Taliesin Chief Poet and you
ran your spear clean into him!

MERLIN *reacts with a great cry, a convulsive arching of the body,
and finally complete rigidity in a corpse-like posture.*

DOCTOR. Aha, you see – I did it! It was the moment for what they
call in Greece the Therapeutic Shock. Herself in there had
done so much for him but it needed the eye of science to know
when and how to complete it. He will recover from his fit shortly
and you'll see he will be just as he was before.

BEDWYR. He'd better be.

DOCTOR. Ah, he will . . .

MERLIN *gradually relaxes.*

MERLIN. And I drove my spear clean into him. A very good place
for it too. Ah yes, I can remember. I can remember why I did it.
Battles – death – catastrophe – it was a very bad reason. The only
true reason to drive a spear at Taliesin is because he was a Chief
Poet just like myself. Or at least, that is what they *thought*. I but
appeared to be a Chief Poet. Inside myself: what was I? I was the
Champion Leaper of this land! Leap out of everything, leap out of
my clothes, leap out of my life –

MORGAN. Leap out of this dirty mill!

He has taken her hand and they execute leaps about the stage – on
MORGAN's *line they both leap together out of sight and they are
heard whooping and laughing away into the distance.*

BEDWYR (*hopelessly running after*). Stop! – My God, we have lost him.

DOCTOR. Ah, to be sure – there was such a case in Egypt last year, I recollect. A fanatical black fellow under the influence of one of those heretic preachers they have there. Sure he jumped into the River Nile and a crocodile took off his legs. In relation to the River *Eden*, there is a boat – it is tied up. If I –

BEDWYR. Doctor, set sail for Connemara whenever you want. You will not be prevented.

DOCTOR. Thank you, Captain. Thank you. (*Exit.*)

BEDWYR (*calling*). The sword!

SCENE TEN

Seascape.

The COMPANIONS *enter. One of them carries* ARTHUR's *sword and hands it to* BEDWYR. BEDWYR *holds it in front of him like a sceptre and paces gravely round the stage – his men following him in a little procession. He arrives at the centre of the stage, holds the sword erect in the position of the Salute, kisses the blade – and then, extending his arm vigorously, he throws the weapon far from him. It vanishes out of sight and there is an appropriate musical accompaniment to its trajectory and its landing in the (unseen) water.*

ANEURIN *has entered on the forestage and he sings while this business is being carried out.*

ANEURIN (*singing*).
    To a deep cold water he carried the sword
    With the strength of his old arm he threw the sword
    The sword will drown and the sword will rust
    And he has obeyed his General's word.
    It was said after that that a hand rose up
    And took the sword and drew it in.
    But this was not true. The sword did drown.
    It was no more than an old man's dream.

BEDWYR *has knelt to pray; the* COMPANIONS *remain standing.*

BEDWYR (*rising to his feet*). So you will turn bandit. You will kill and you will rob.

FIRST COMPANION. What else is there left?

BEDWYR. You will not be prevented by me.

Exeunt BEDWYR *and* COMPANIONS *severally.*

SCENE ELEVEN

Ruins.

ANEURIN (*singing*).
> I did not know where Merlin Poet
> Had gone and I did not try to inquire:
> I took his wife and she took me to her bed
> For love and for pity and also for desire . . .

> GWENDDYDD *is carrying various bundles of luggage. She makes up a rough bed of blankets on the forestage.*

GWENDDYDD. What else is there left . . . ? Do you know what you have done?

ANEURIN. Something I should not, I have no doubt? What is it, love? Tell me.

GWENDDYDD. You have put a baby in my womb.

ANEURIN. No.

GWENDDYDD. Oh yes, you have. You did and no one else. A bit of a bad mistake, isn't it?

ANEURIN. Indeed not.

GWENDDYDD. But where shall we live? What are we going to eat?

ANEURIN. Ah, we will discover something. In the meantime we won't worry. The winter, thank God, is over – we have a tent, more or less waterproof, we have found a valley in which to pitch it where the landscape is full of flowers and the people are not hostile, and best of all, I have found myself a job of work. I assist the blacksmith in his forge – I can blow his bellows, hold out his tongs for him – it is not what you'd call a *skill*, but it is rewarded by bowls of porridge and now and again a piece of beef. Moreover, his wife is kind and she has promised to take care of you. We won't worry. (*He kisses her. She responds, but then draws back.*)

GWENDDYDD. How often do you ask yourself – who takes care of Merlin?

ANEURIN. I don't ask myself that question. He ran off hand-in-hand with Morgan, and they –

GWENDDYDD. Morgan is dead.

ANEURIN. Who told you that?

GWENDDYDD. The blacksmith.

ANEURIN. He didn't tell me.

GWENDDYDD. No, love – you work for him. But I am his friend. He said that when the snow melted, at the bottom of a great cliff, about twenty miles out of Carlisle, a shepherd-boy one morning came upon Morgan's body. The rural people had seen both Merlin and herself laughing and leaping across the ridges of the hill. They were in competition with one another like a pair of excited puppydogs, which could go the fastest. It is thought she went too fast, she went over the edge. 'God help us, but at her age to put forward so much mad spirit!' That's what the wife of the blacksmith said – she said, 'God help us, that old Morgan, she was the queen of the heart of the lot of us'. And so Merlin is left alone.

ANEURIN. Which is all that he had need of. So that's it ... We don't ask questions (*He kisses her again and they snuggle down into the blankets.*)

> *Enter* MERLIN, *creeping stooped over, his hands down by his ankles, like a bird with folded wings. He is now – and until the end of the play – wearing his second Mad Outfit. This consists of a mask considerably less realistic than his previous one – the face is green and gold and the hair and beard – very long – are dark green and blue-black. His body-stocking is green, and where before there were tufts of black hair there are now also feathers of various shining colours. (Note. The mask might very well be shaped into something of a beaked bird-like quality.)*

MERLIN.
> The men and women of this world
> Walk on two legs and grunt and squeal.
> Merlin enjoys the noise they make

But he prefers
The crying of the birds
Until such time
As he can find
Beneath the roof of close mankind
Room for two wings as well as for two feet.
Meanwhile he will waste words
Upon the screaming birds
And he will wait
Until a starling or a nightingale
Will fly to London or to cold Carlisle
And tell the men who swarm there what he said.
By which time Merlin very likely will be dead.

And yet there is a strange thing . . . Morgan has gone and I don't
know where she went. She was laughing and running and jumping with me in the fog – and then suddenly dead silence and I
have never heard her nor seen her since. No . . . not alone Morgan.
Who was the other one . . . ? I remember someone else – but there
is a fog all over it . . . what . . . ? I remember a young woman . . . I
remember her body as though I had lived in it . . . I don't remember her name . . .

*He prowls about, struggling in his mind. Then it comes to him and
he lets out a shout of triumphant recollection.*

Gwenddydd –!
  (*He sings.*)
Through all of Cumbria and Strathclyde
And all the woods of Caledonia
I will crawl and I will slide
I will nose out my road
Until I come to her!

TALIESIN *suddenly appears and obstructs the passage of* MERLIN.
TALIESIN *is wearing a long blue tunic, or shift, with an enormous
blood-red and pus-yellow stain upon it. He has on a mask which is
a monstrous caricature of his own face – all distorted into a
grimace of pain with a wide-open mouth: the principal colour of
the mask is white with grey patches. He holds his poet's staff in
front of* MERLIN.

TALIESIN (*chanting*).

Merlin, my curse is not yet taken off.
Seek in your deep dream for the kindness of your wife –
You will find me and no one else
And I will bar your way.
I am the head of Taliesin
And the wide wound you made so red –
All the rest of me is no more than an old man on his death-bed:
But I am the wound and the head
And I am here in the wood –

MERLIN *endeavours stubbornly to force his way past.*

Merlin, it is far better you should turn back
Your wife is asleep
She will not wake
She does not sleep alone –

MERLIN *wrestles with him.*

Merlin I have cursed you
It is far better you should be gone –!

MERLIN *overcomes* TALIESIN *and sends him spinning, right off the stage.*

MERLIN.

I have not gone.
I have not been afraid.

He comes down forestage, to the bed.

To the side of my bright lady
At last I have made my way.

GWENDDYDD *stirs in her sleep and then sits up slowly, looking at* MERLIN *as though she saw him in her dreams.*

Bright lady, you rest easy
In the bed with your new lover,
It is not so with me.
I am your cold and lonely rover,
That sharp-beaked clown one full September
Who toppled you over and over
Where the marshland was wet and muddy

And the grasshoppers were full of thunder.
I gave you a great stroke down your body
A bleeding stroke with my yellow claw –
Neither bird nor man did ever espy
From the height of the sky
So desirable and easy a bed
As the one you sleep in now.

GWENDDYDD.
Merlin, it is not so easy as you may believe it to be –
Knowing only your own bed alone in the top of the tree.
Not so easy but more welcome
Come enter it, my ruined husband.

MERLIN.
No, for the young man in it
Is neither ruined nor does he deserve it.
He remained constant from the day of his birth
To the wild forest and the rain-soaked earth.
I, in my youth, ran shamefully for shelter.
Now, in my prime, I am out and I must wander.
I came only to look at you and to endeavour to remember.

GWENDDYDD.
If you will not creep under the blanket
And sleep with us safe and sound
I must put out my own foot and set it on the ground –

She does so. She takes his hand.

I will run with you and fly with you
Wing against wing:
From my breast and my round shoulders
Bright feathers will spring,
Soft down upon my belly will grow and –
Oh God, but I can't. Bring forth a child in the woods and not
your child –! Oh what is to be done . . . ?

She sinks back upon the bed and buries her face in her hands.

MERLIN (*withdrawing a little but gazing at her intently, he sings*).
One night I was beside the River Clyde
Another at the Liddel waterside.
Penrith I knew, Caerlaverock I visited
Upon the hill of Caerlanrigg I would lie and I would sit.

Upon the open field of Camlann where the bones are white
I stood and sang for my lost love all night.

BLACKSMITH'S VOICE (*offstage*). Hello, hello, hello there –!

MERLIN *escapes very rapidly.* GWENDDYDD *and* ANEURIN
wake up. The BLACKSMITH *runs in.*

BLACKSMITH. Gwenddydd, Aneurin Poet – you must pick up your
gear and go. There has word come to the valley that the English
are upon the move!

ANEURIN. All of them?

BLACKSMITH. Not yet but there are enough – a war-party, five
hundred men, across the headwaters of Tyne and of Tweed,
burning every habitation, and the blood upon their swords as
ever – God, but there is no Army to give us any kind of defence!
I have the oxen put to the yoke and the wagon loaded up with
everything out of the forge. You must come with us to save your
lives – all *three* of you – come!

GWENDDYDD. Come with you where?

BLACKSMITH. West, into the land of Galloway. Heathen people.
Dangerous.

ANEURIN. It is a chance.

GWENDDYDD. We have to take it.

BLACKSMITH. We have to take it at this moment. In God's name
we have no time to waste. (*He helps them get together their gear and
hurries them off.*)

SCENE TWELVE

Raid.

ANEURIN (*re-enters singing*).
It was in such fear that we set out
For Galloway – a fugitive
Dare not expect wherever he goes
The men of that land will let him live.
Two-thirds of the men of every land
Are fugitives in this murderous age.

We were more fortunate than most,
The men of Galloway did not rage –
– rather they received us with a kind of generous despair. They did beg from us one thing: 'Do not bring your bad customs into our unfortunate land.' And we did not. We abided by their own customs – both bad and good. When Gwenddydd gave birth to her baby it proved to be a daughter. In those parts it is the women who are accorded the inheritance, so this was good. We gave her the name of Blodeuwedd, which means 'Girl-made-out-of-flowers' – though it seems to me that thorns had quite as much as flowers to do with her conception. A long long time afterwards I heard what had happened to the man who could have been her father – were it not for those thorns. All he had need of was to be left alone – indeed yes, but I was not thinking then he would be left alone in the midst of this . . . (*He indicates the 'Raid' scene now lit by the glare of flames.*)

MERLIN, *furtive and frightened, comes across the stage.*

ANEURIN (*singing*).
A poet alone in the dark forest
May learn once more how to be a poet.
There are others alone in the dark forest
But they will be killed if they dare to come out.

A group of PEASANT REFUGEES, *men and women, carrying bundles of household effects, etc., and including the* COWMAN *and the* COWMAN'S WIFE, *enter from different directions and stand in a forlorn huddle.* MERLIN *has fled again at their approach. Enter* BEDWYR, *dressed in rough sackcloth and barefoot.*

BEDWYR. Good people, we are safe here, take rest, and do not reproach me. It is no fault of my own that when the English set fire to your houses there was no one to prevent it.

COWMAN. Then whose fault was it – Captain of Carlisle?

BEDWYR. You are not to use those words!

ANOTHER REFUGEE. Whose fault was it?

BEDWYR. The Hand of God. His chastisement. Innocent you are, all of you; but all the land has been chastised. And we must learn to comprehend it. Here in the forest we will establish our new community. It will be such hard work, we have so little left, so many trees will have to be cut down before anything can be planted. But we will work under the battle-standard of our Lord Jesus Christ: and the first building that we set up will be a decent little chapel made of timber and turf, and every day the bell will ring and the Miracle of the Mass, the Body and Blood of God, will be set forth for our redemption.

Dear brothers and sisters in Christ – do not ever again call me Captain of Carlisle. I have told you I am ordained Priest at the hands of a most venerable Bishop: the weapons of my old warfare are gone down into deep water. Your protection from this time on is the Love of God and nothing else. With the help of God I will provide it.

> *They all sit.* BEDWYR *distributes food, breaking bread and passing round a jug of milk.*

ANEURIN. And so they lived in the forest and Bedwyr became a Saint and they worked and they prospered – until in the end they were almost free from fear. The English are no longer a danger to them – the English have taken what they want and that is all.

SCENE THIRTEEN

Woodland.

MERLIN *enters, well upstage.*

ANEURIN (*continuing*).
> But who is this man by day and night
> Who in and out at the edge of the wood
> Fixes his wild dark eyes upon
> The gentle work of the people of God?

> *The* REFUGEES *go out to their work, leaving only* BEDWYR *and the* COWMAN'S WIFE.

COWMAN'S WIFE. My husband has not yet seen him. He is altogether too busy looking after the cattle. But I have seen him many times. Holy Father, I am terrified.

BEDWYR. My daughter, there is no need. I know who he is. He

wants to talk to us, that is all. You see, he renounced God and he
knows that his soul is forfeit.

COWMAN'S WIFE. He renounced God!

BEDWYR. In effect. But God will reach out to him, the Shepherd's
Crook will hook his leg, he will be brought back into the flock.
There is nothing to prevent it, now that Taliesin is dead . . .
Look you, daughter, the poor creature is first of all in need of
food. Do you think you could provide for him?

COWMAN'S WIFE. Oh, Holy Father – no –! Inside my hut – a fear-
ful thing like that –!

BEDWYR. I did not say inside the hut. Put some milk for him, at
nightfall, quite close to the gate of the fold-yard. He will come
and he will take it; and then, one day, he will come and talk. I
will then be able to tell him all the truth of the Love of God. Do
what I ask, it is not dangerous. You need never meet the man at
all. Indeed, I will go further: you are not to meet the man at all,
neither meet with him nor speak with him – until you have spoken
to me. You understand me, my child?

Exit BEDWYR. *The* COWMAN'S WIFE *carries out the action
described in the following song – as does* MERLIN.

ANEURIN (*singing*).
    So every night with her nervous foot
    She drove a little hole in the ground –
    She poured in the milk and Merlin came
    And he knelt and he lapped up the milk like a hound.
    And then one night he decided to talk
    She was so frightened she could hardly stand
    In front of the naked man in the dark
    Who caught her and held her with his hand.

MERLIN *has come suddenly upon her, after he has finished the
milk. She has been watching him drink from what seems a safe
distance. He has hold of her kerchief knot under her chin.*

MERLIN. I want to sing to you.

COWMAN'S WIFE (*in a terrified whisper*). Oh God –

MERLIN. Don't make a noise or they will come and interrupt me . . .

*He releases her and stands back a little. She is too scared to cry
out, but watches him with a growing fascination.*

They will haul me in to Jesus and I do not want to go. I know more about Jesus than any of them do. Jesus ran through the forest, stark crazy, making poems. And because he could not find any man or woman to hear his poems, had himself spiked up in public on the wide branches of a tree so that no one would ever be able to say they did not know he had ever lived! Merlin will not do that. Merlin has learned better. You are a good woman. I have been watching you; the work that you do is good –

> All this year all by myself
> In a world that to other men appears to be quite empty
> I have watched and I have seen so many things of such beauty –
> But not even the beauty and revelation of the rainbow
> Was as bright in my sight as the line of milk that you draw
> From the udder of your cow.

And has one single poet ever thought to ask you what kind of song he ought to make? No. I am asking, now. You tell me. I will make it.

COWMAN'S WIFE. I – I – please go away.

MERLIN. Ah, you can't tell me –

ANEURIN (*addressing the audience from the corner of the forestage*). What I said to Bedwyr about the loneliness of the poet is not true!

MERLIN. I ought to have known. I took you by surprise . . .

ANEURIN. I told Bedwyr a stupid lie because I was frightened . . .

MERLIN. But none the less I will sing to you . . .

ANEURIN. The poet without the people is nothing. The people without the poet will still be the people . . .

MERLIN. To you, and for you, and for your husband and for your children . . .

ANEURIN. All that we can do is to make loud and to make clear their own proper voice. They have so much to say . . .

MERLIN. I know about your children. I have been watching them. Look, I brought some blackberries. You give them when I'm gone.

ANEURIN. An impediment in their speech they may very well have, but – Mother of God – they are not dumb!

COWMAN'S WIFE. Very early for blackberries, isn't it? We didn't find any yet . . .

MERLIN. Ssh – ssh – here is the song. (*He sings.*)

> Mother of your children
> And wife of your good man

Your face is pale with terror
But you stand up tall and strong.
The green man from the thorny wood
Wears neither wool nor silk
But his chest is broad and his eyes are clear –
He has drunk your good white milk.

COWMAN'S WIFE. If you had a bit of good brown bread to go with
it, it would do you no harm. Wait – there is a new loaf. I have just
taken it out of the coals –

MERLIN. No – not yet – I must finish the song. The song is for your
pleasure – out of gratitude – please listen to it.

COWMAN'S WIFE. It is a pleasure to *you* to be singing it, I think.
You don't look to be a fellow who ever had that much pleasure.
No business of mine to pull it away from you. Go on, boy – do
you sing.

MERLIN. I will not. You are laughing at me.

COWMAN'S WIFE. Smiling – and why not?

MERLIN. Smiling and why not? By God but I will make a verse
about the way your mouth turns up – (*He sings.*)

It came so quick it came so warm
Across your face of fear
As a man might see on a frozen moor
The running of the wild red deer.

Now look, you can fetch me the bread. But just to prove to me
one thing. That you did not think to get it because the Saint put
it into your mind.

COWMAN'S WIFE. You silly man, of course he didn't.

MERLIN.

Ah, but there was a time when I deemed the yelp of the wolf-
pack
To be more melodious by far
Than the bleat like a sheep of a little clergyman in his church –
Baa – baa baa – baa –

COWMAN'S WIFE. Ssh – the Saint will hear you I doubt if he'd care
to be laughed at, even by a lunatic.

But she is laughing too. MERLIN *bleats again and they both laugh
in a warm friendliness.*
Enter the COWMAN *surreptitiously. He has a short spear in his
hand.*

COWMAN. I can think of but one business that a naked man at sunset should have with my wife at the back of my hut . . .

MERLIN (*stops laughing and sings, with great joy*).
> O the running of the deer
> And the beating of my heart –
> I am welcome at last for the man that I am
> And neither for craft nor art!

The COWMAN *drives his spear into* MERLIN.

COWMAN'S WIFE. Oh Jesus, Jesus, Jesus – what is it you have done –!

BEDWYR *and the* REFUGEES *come running in.*

BEDWYR. The Curse of Christ upon you, cowherd. Were it not for your crazy jealousy I would have had this man for Christ.

MERLIN *bleats derisively, and dies.*

Nevertheless I do pronounce that Merlin died at peace with God. Any poet that tells it different shall stand condemned as an enemy of the truth.

He kneels down beside the body and prays. During the following song the people prepare the body for burial and carry it away.

ANEURIN (*singing*).
> There was a man called Lazarus
> And when he died they said he died at peace with God.
> They had muffled a rag round his open mouth
> And as he died he could not speak one word.
> Perhaps he tried but he was not heard.
> Then a fool of a friend, who did not know
> When to be quiet or loud, into the graveyard ran –
> He danced on the grave in great big boots –
> 'O Lazarus, Lazarus, are you awake, young man?
> Come out of there, come up, come on –!'
> The clay did heave and the clay did hoist
> And Lazarus he came up like a strange gigantic mole.
> He tore the muffler from his jaw –
> All rotten he was, with such an evil smell
> They closed their eyes and down they fell.

And this is what Lazarus said to them all
When he came back to life so hideous and so tall:
'O I found underground
A score or two
Of decent people
Just like you.
I found underground
Two thousand or three
Of stinking corpses
Just like me.
And when the big boots
Dance on the grave
It is the corpses
They will raise
For you went and you buried them
With all the life inside
That they could not live
While they were alive.
We are going to come back
And we are going to take hold
So hideous and bloody greedy
We take hold of the whole world!'

Exit.

TRANSLATION OF PHRASES AND SENTENCES QUOTED IN LATIN AND ANGLO SAXON

p. 34

MEDRAUT. I understand your instructions and will obey.

BEDWYR and COMPANIONS. We understand your instructions and will obey.

MEDRAUT. Each man to his duty – go.

p. 83

BEDWYR. Bugler, sound the recall.

BEDWYR. Prepare to move off in column of route.

p. 84

ARTHUR. Set forward the banner.

BEDWYR. The banner is set forward, General. To your horses – prepare to mount.

p. 110

MEDRAUT (*to the* ENGLISHMAN). What is the name of your war-leader?

ENGLISHMAN. Ida, son of Eoppa –

ENGLISHMAN. Son of Esa, son of Ingwy, son of Angenwit, son of Alloc, son of –

p. 111

MEDRAUT. When did you get this letter?

ENGLISHMAN. Before we set sail from Germany.

A COMPANION. I understand your instructions and will obey.

p. 114

MEDRAUT. I understand your instructions and will obey.

p. 138

MEDRAUT. The General is going to send you back to your war-leader.

MEDRAUT. The General says you have a right to be here. It would not be honourable for him to make war on you.

ENGLISHMAN. All Welshmen are without honour, but every one of you will be killed!

p. 216

BEDWYR. Obey my orders!

FIRST COMPANION (*after a pause*). We understand your instructions and will obey.

Methuen's Modern Plays

EDITED BY JOHN CULLEN AND GEOFFREY STRACHAN

Paul Ableman	*Green Julia*
Jean Anouilh	*Antigone*
	Becket
	Poor Bitos
	Ring Round the Moon
	The Lark
	The Rehearsal
	The Fighting Cock
	Dear Antoine
	The Director of the Opera
John Arden	*Serjeant Musgrave's Dance*
	The Workhouse Donkey
	Armstrong's Last Goodnight
	Left-Handed Liberty
	Soldier, Soldier and Other Plays
	Two Autobiographical Plays
John Arden and	*The Business of Good Government*
Margaretta D'Arcy	*The Royal Pardon*
	The Hero Rises Up
Ayckbourn, Bowen,	*Mixed Doubles*
Brook, Campton,	
Melly, Owen, Pinter,	
Saunders, Weldon	
Brendan Behan	*The Quare Fellow*
	The Hostage
	Richard's Cork Leg
Barry Bermange	*No Quarter and the Interview*
Edward Bond	*Saved*
	Narrow Road to the Deep North
	The Pope's Wedding
	Lear
	The Sea
	Bingo
John Bowen	*Little Boxes*
	The Disorderly Women